MARIA'S KEEPERS

By the same author

The Most Evil of Them All – When narcissism turns deadly

MARIA'S KEEPERS

One woman's escape from the Jehovah's Witnesses Church in South Africa

SAM HUMAN

PENGUIN BOOKS

Maria's Keepers

Published by Penguin Books
an imprint of Penguin Random House (Pty) Ltd
Company Reg. No. 1953/000441/07
The Estuaries No. 4, Oxbow Crescent, Century Avenue, Century City, Cape Town, 7441
www.penguinrandomhouse.co.za

Penguin Random House South Africa

First published 2024

1 3 5 7 9 10 8 6 4 2

PUBLISHER: Marlene Fryer
MANAGING EDITOR: Ronel Richter-Herbert
PROOFREADER: Tracy Murinik
COVER AND TEXT DESIGNER: Ryan Africa
TYPESETTER: Monique van den Berg

Set in 11.5 pt on 15.5 pt Adobe Caslon Pro

Printed by ***novus print***, a division of Novus Holdings

FSC www.fsc.org
MIX
Paper | Supporting responsible forestry
FSC® C022948

ISBN 978 1 77639 135 6 (print)
ISBN 978 1 77639 136 3 (ePub)

Contents

DISCLAIMER

The contents of this book are the opinion of the author, based on the recollections of the personal experiences of the main character of this narrative (Maria), as well as thorough research using materials sourced in the public domain. All efforts have been made to relay only accurate information. Quotes and references have been provided to back up the views herein.

Author's note: All names, including Maria's, and place names in this story have been changed to protect the privacy of the main character and all those associated with her story. The intention of this book is only to share her experience of growing up in the Jehovah's Witnesses Church in South Africa.

Acknowledgements

Samantha

To my editor, Ronel Richter-Herbert from Penguin Random House South Africa, thank you for your guidance, advice and constant support, not to mention your good humour under pressure. Thank you.

To my parents, Paula and Lesley, for your unconditional love and for the immense privilege of having had a happy and stable childhood. And to Laurentius, Taicla and Josh, for your constant encouragement and support, as well as your ever-helpful constructive criticism – you are my world.

Finally, to 'Maria', for your courage and strength to stand up and speak out. I hope this book does your story the justice it deserves and that your message reaches those who need it most.

Maria

To my husband, thank you for always being so supportive and loving throughout this journey; you have been my rock.

To Samantha Human, thank you for listening and translating my past into a book that people can read – it has been the greatest pleasure.

To all who are trapped and feel alone in the Jehovah's Witnesses Church, I hope this book gives you the strength to find a way out and the courage to leave.

Escape

She came … she conquered … she took their advice
To change her life … she'd have to pay a price
She DID … she conquered … she still stands waiting
For an artificial picture that no one is painting

In a crowded church, inside she screams …
Wishing someone would notice her call & fulfil her dreams
Her call for LIFE … her call for ACCEPTANCE … her call for
HAPPINESS that doesn't involve repentance!

So, they stand, they judge, they turn their heads
She stands … she cries … hanging on very few threads
No one notices nor does anyone care,
But only when she leaves the religion, it raises people's hair

She rocks herself to sleep at night
Knowing that what they've done to her is not all right
Telling herself everything will be fine,
But in the end, those very thoughts are mine

The choices I make are now my own,
So don't pretend you're better than me … sitting on your throne!
She came … she conquered … she REJECTED their advice,
To change her life … she'd still have to pay the ultimate price.

– Maria

Abbreviations and Glossary of Terms

Anointed 144 000
Jehovah's Witnesses believe that while the majority of Jehovah's Witnesses will live forever in an earthly paradise, 144 000 have been specifically selected to ascend to heaven in order to sit at Jehovah God's 'right hand' and rule with Christ.

Apostate
An ex-Witness who speaks out publicly against the organisation.

Armageddon
A battle between the forces of God and Satan that the Jehovah's Witnesses believe to be imminent. During the battle, the 'wicked' non–Jehovah's Witnesses on earth will be destroyed and the planet given over to the faithful (Jehovah's Witnesses) as an earthly paradise in which they will live forever.

Baptism
The act of dedicating your life to Jehovah through the sacrament of baptism.

Bethel
Watch Tower Society's headquarters and publishing factory in New York (United States). Bethel is staffed entirely by volunteers called Bethelites. The workers are fed, sheltered and given a very small stipend in exchange for printing Jehovah's Witnesses' literature.

Disassociation
This occurs when a baptised Witness leaves the congregation of his or her own volition. Disassociated Witnesses are shunned.

Disfellowshipping
The act of removing a believer from the rolls of the organisation for violating certain doctrines of the Watch Tower Society. The disfellowshipped member is shunned.

Field Service
Going door to door, preaching.

Jehovah's Witnesses (abbreviated to JWs or Witnesses)
A sect of Christians who follow the millennial teachings of Charles Taze Russell. Abbreviated to JW. The Witnesses believe that the true name of God and the only name he recognises is 'Jehovah'.

Kingdom Hall
A place of worship used by Jehovah's Witnesses.

Pioneer
A person dedicated to the field-service ministry full time.

Publisher
A person who goes door to door for a minimum of ten hours every month. (A pioneer goes in service for a minimum of ninety hours per month.)

Watch Tower Bible and Tract Society (abbreviated to WTS)
Originally the Bible Students founded by Charles Taze Russell in 1881. The WTS is the driving force behind the doctrines of the Kingdom Hall of Jehovah's Witnesses and the publisher of *The Watchtower* and *Awake!* magazines. Its headquarters are in New York.

Watchtower/Watch Tower Society
Shortened names for the Watch Tower Bible and Tract Society.

The Watchtower* and *Awake!
Biweekly magazines published by the Watch Tower Society for the edification of Witnesses as well as the general public. They are written by the Bethelite staff of the Watch Tower Bible and Tract Society.

The Truth
The beliefs of Jehovah's Witnesses. You are either 'in the Truth' or 'outside of the Truth'. Occasionally, the Watch Tower Society receives 'new light' from Jehovah, and the 'human' stewards and elders of Jehovah then report this new information to all Witnesses, worldwide, who then adjust their beliefs going forward.

Worldly
Anyone who is not of the Jehovah's Witnesses faith.

Who are Jehovah and His Witnesses?

'We worship the one true and Almighty God, the Creator, whose name is Jehovah, God of Abraham, Moses, and Jesus. We follow the teachings and example of Jesus Christ and honour him as our Saviour and the Son of God. We are thus Christians. The Kingdom of God is a real government in heaven, not a condition in the hearts of Christians. Soon it will replace human governments and accomplish God's purpose for earth ...'
– Jehovah's Witnesses.org (JW.org),
the official website for the Jehovah's Witnesses Church

God's purpose? According to Jehovah's Witnesses, it is the total obliteration of humankind as we know it, sparing only the most faithful Witnesses and heralding a new dawn of human civilisation in a 'cleansed' earthly paradise. This is the bedrock on which the church of Jehovah's Witnesses is built and the doctrine by which all who serve Jehovah abide. To understand this prophecy is to understand the Jehovah's Witnesses Church and its followers.

The name Jehovah is derived from ancient Hebrew; in the Hebrew Bible, the name for God is יהוה (*YHWH*). As no vowels appear in the word, the earliest pronunciation, by inserting vowels, became 'Yahweh', with a second pronunciation, 'Yehovah', commonly translated as 'Jehovah'. For Jehovah's Witnesses, Jehovah is not interchangeable with the term God, nor do they refer to 'God'; they refer only to Jehovah or Jehovah God.

According to the official website for Jehovah's Witnesses – JW.org – the Bible prophesises that humans are living in the 'last days', and that the end of human existence as we know it is imminent. Armageddon is real and close. This prophecy has been in existence for over a hundred years. According to Jehovah's Witnesses, Jesus is the only son of Jehovah God and is destined to reign as King in Jehovah's Kingdom in heaven. His 'rule' began in the year 1914, and the doomsday clock has been ticking ever since.

You might be wondering why Jesus only started 'ruling' in 1914 specifically, nearly 2 000 years after his death in AD 30 in Jerusalem during ancient Roman rule. What has occupied Jesus for the previous two millennia?

Most Christian-based faiths believe that after Jesus was crucified and died on the cross, he rose from the dead and ascended to heaven to rejoin God the Father as a united entity, reigning as King in heaven and watching over 'his flock'. This event is known to all Christians as the Ascension of Jesus Christ, significant for its depiction of Jesus's ability to defy death and resurrect his physical body from the dead.

Jehovah's Witnesses, however, believe that Jesus is Jehovah God's only begotten son, and they regard him as a separate entity to Jehovah. When Jesus died, his spirit, and not his physical body, was resurrected, and he only took his rightful place in Jehovah's Kingdom in the year 1914.

But why only in 1914, approximately 2 000 years after his passing? According to Jehovah's Witnesses, Jerusalem had always been the capital city of the Jewish nation – the seat of rule of the line of kings from the House of King David. They sat on 'Jehovah's throne' as representatives of God himself, making Jerusalem a symbol of Jehovah's rule. But when the Babylonians conquered Jerusalem in 607 BCE, God's rule in Jerusalem was crushed.

'Jehovah's throne' was left vacant, and the line of kings who descended from David was interrupted. But this 'trampling of the throne' would not go on forever. 'The one who has the legal right to the Davidic crown is Christ Jesus. So, the "trampling" would end when Jesus became King,' claims JW.org.

In fact, this 'big reveal' would only take place some 2 520 years later, in October 1914, according to JW.org: 'At this time, the appointed times of the nations ended, and Jesus Christ was installed as God's heavenly King and thus [began] "the last days" of this present wicked system of things.'

Jehovah's Witnesses further claim that Jehovah God, Jesus Christ and the faithful angels all reside in the spirit realm, and that a relatively small number of people – or 144 000 to be exact – will be resurrected to live in heaven after 'the end of days', and rule with Jesus in Jehovah's Kingdom.

This figure is derived from a literal interpretation of the Book of Revelation, verse 7:14, which states that only 144 000 of the elect elite will be called to heaven. The remaining faithful (Jehovah's Witnesses) will live forever in a renewed earthly paradise in newly resurrected bodies. These faithful individuals will be blessed with everlasting life, while the 144 000 'chosen elite' will reside in heaven. This, of course, only after Jehovah has annihilated the rest of the 8 billion unworthy people residing on the planet.

There is a glimmer of hope, however, because if one reads on, JW.org says: 'God intends to bring billions back from death by means of a resurrection. However, those who refuse to learn God's ways after being raised to life will be destroyed forever with no hope of a resurrection.'

Thus, after suffering through the first wave of human annihilation, one might be able to redeem and save oneself by way of a miraculous epiphany of remorse, repentance and conversion to Jehovah's teachings. For the rest of the world's mere mortals, anyone who is not a Jehovah's Witness or a reformed, repentant one – especially atheists, agnostics and evolutionists – there appears only one outcome: eternal damnation and obliteration. The first sequel of Armageddon is an opportunity at a second chance, to rethink one's choices – but if you make the wrong choice, there is no second act.

These are harsh warnings for humankind, and if you are a Witness to Jehovah, they are not to be taken lightly. In fact, these prophecies are the foundation on which every Witness pledges their unconditional and uncompromising allegiance to the Kingdom of Jehovah. The very same foundation on which the true-life story of this book's protagonist, Maria, is based – a harrowing tale of clandestine family manipulation, emotional imprisonment and alleged sexual abuse by senior members of a South African chapter of the global conglomerate that is the Jehovah's Witnesses Church, headquartered in New York in the United States.

American author Hemant Mehta, the editor of FriendlyAtheist.com, explains in the foreword of *The Reluctant Apostate: Leaving Jehovah's Witnesses Comes at a Price*, that for a long time his understanding of Jehovah's Witnesses' beliefs 'boiled down to kind of Christian, but with a few quirks. I knew they didn't accept blood transfusions. That was probably the worst of it. I could not have been more ignorant.'

It was only in recent years that Mehta learnt about apostasy trials, the practice of disfellowshipping members, Jehovah's Witnesses' criticism of higher education, their claims that the theory of evolution is a conspiracy, and instances of alleged cover-ups and denials of systemic sexual abuse and homophobia.

As Lloyd Evans writes in *The Reluctant Apostate*: 'I had no idea Witnesses felt love was conditional. Forget the idea of blood being thicker than water. If you dare to disagree about Jehovah, that blood loses its viscosity in a heartbeat. Sons and daughters become dead to the very people who gave them life, and moms and dads are treated as invisible by those whom they cradled in their arms as babies.'

Against a backdrop of selfless love and a seemingly benign, unconditional serving of God, there are former Jehovah's Witnesses who have left the church, and attest to a vastly different reality to that portrayed on the official Jehovah's Witnesses website. One such person is Maria, a former Jehovah's Witness in South Africa, whose story may resonate with current or former Witnesses. Shamed and ostracised by her family and her congregation for not only questioning her faith, but also for standing up against the sexual abuse she endured by the very people she 'served' and respected, she was eventually excommunicated from her faith and shunned by her family.

Of the many double standards that she was forced to tolerate, Maria's experiences of sexual abuse and emotional 'gaslighting' at the hands of senior members of her community church are by far the most distressing. These were 'crimes' for which she was not only shamed, but also blamed. Sadly, Maria's experiences are not necessarily unique. A damning 2016 report by the Australian Royal Commission into 'Institutional Responses to Child Sex Abuse' revealed evidence from case files held by the Jehovah's Witnesses organisation that recorded allegations, reports or complaints of child sexual abuse by 1006 members of the organisation.

The Royal Commission found that children and young adults within the JW organisation are not adequately protected from the risk of child sexual abuse; that the organisation does not respond adequately to allegations of child sexual abuse; and, given their outdated internal disciplinary procedures, for the most part, are lacking in their understanding of what constitutes sexual abuse.

The Royal Commission also found that the Jehovah's Witnesses organisation's internal disciplinary system for addressing complaints of child sexual abuse was not child or survivor focused. 'Survivors are offered little or no choice in how their complaint is addressed, sanctions are weak, with little regard to the risk of the perpetrator reoffending.'

Finally, the Royal Commission considered the organisation's general practice of not reporting serious instances of child sexual abuse to authorities demonstrated a serious failure to provide for the safety and protection of children.

Similarly, Maria's story reflects the failure of her Jehovah's Witnesses congregation to respond adequately and compassionately to her claims of abuse and mistreatment, driving her to a state of desperate unhappiness, angst and isolation.

A *BBC News* report in February 2020 revealed that twenty former Jehovah's Witnesses were suing the church in the United Kingdom over historical sexual abuse, with one former elder claiming that the church had failed to ever involve the authorities.

The report claimed that the Jehovah's Witnesses' policy of not punishing alleged child sex abusers unless a second person, in addition to the accuser, has also witnessed the event (known as the two-witness rule), or unless the abuser openly confesses (unlikely, of course), to be problematic.

The official response to this report from the Jehovah's Witnesses camp was that its elders do comply with child-abuse reporting laws, even if there is only one witness present, and that they always notify the police if a child is in danger, which the former elder of the church vehemently denied, accusing the church of failing to involve the authorities over many years.

According to the *BBC News* report: 'John Viney, the former elder, says he was himself abused between the ages of nine and thirteen, by a distant family member who was an active Jehovah's Witness: "I know for a fact now that there are parents that haven't done anything about the abuse of their children by others because they don't want to bring reproach on Jehovah's name."'

This former elder's daughter was also abused as a child and has since spoken about it publicly. When she left the church, her father disowned her, something he has regretted ever since: 'When I was an elder and a dad, I put being an elder absolutely first.'

In 2019, *Rolling Stone* magazine reported on a 2019 report by a US-based magazine and multi-platform publisher, *The Atlantic*, that alleged the existence of a decades-old database of accused paedophiles within the Jehovah's Witnesses organisation that had been withheld from authorities for years. This database is said to contain thousands of names and addresses of accused child molesters within the church, as well as detailed reports of the specific allegations against them.

The database was thought to have been prompted by a 1997 letter that the Watch Tower Bible and Tract Society sent to all congregations within the US, instructing their leaders to document all known abuse allegations and their alleged perpetrators, and to send the report back to Watch Tower in a sealed envelope without informing the authorities. These letters were then reportedly used to compile an in-house database of known perpetrators within the US chapters of the organisation.

In its response to *The Atlantic*'s report, the Watch Tower's Office of Public Information claimed that their policies on child protection comply with the law, including any requirement to report allegations of child abuse to authorities. According to *The Atlantic*, the existence of the database was made public in 2012, when a man named Jose Lopez filed a lawsuit alleging that he had been sexually abused at the age of seven by an adult church member named Gonzalo Campos in one of the San Diego chapters of the organisation. Although Lopez's mother reportedly informed the church elders of the abuse, they failed to inform the police, allegedly citing their 'two-witness rule', whereby two witnesses are required to substantiate a claim of sexual abuse.

Arguably, the suitability of this rule in the context of child sexual abuse is questionable given that any sexual abuse invariably occurs in private, where the only witnesses to the abuse are the perpetrator and the victim. *Reveal*, an investigative news agency representing The Center for Investigative Reporting (CIR), a non-profit investigative journalism and multimedia news platform, founded in the United States in 1977, has followed this particular story for several years and provides corroborating information. They report that after years of litigation, Lopez's case against the Watch Tower Bible and Tract Society was eventually settled out of court in March 2018 for an undisclosed amount. (This outcome was also covered in a *San Diego*

Union-Tribune article, dated 6 March 2019, and titled 'San Diego Sex Abuse Cases Against Jehovah's Witness Organisation Settled', as well as in *The San Diego Reader*, dated 12 January 2018, and titled: 'Jehovah's Witnesses to Settle Sex Abuse Case'.)

In a previous 2015 court decision, a San Diego state judge ruled that Watch Tower had failed to co-operate with discovery in the Lopez case and awarded him an amount of $13.5 million. Watch Tower appealed the case, and the award was rescinded on the condition that they hand over the documents that allegedly detailed the organisation's knowledge of child sex abuse, going back decades across their congregations in the US. The court said that Watch Tower would be heavily penalised if they refused to do so, and in 2016, they acquiesced and began handing over documents to Irwin Zalkin, the attorney representing the plaintiff, Jose Lopez.

Watch Tower were said to have provided the documents on condition that they were placed under a protective order, meaning Zalkin could not discuss their contents or share them with law-enforcement agencies, reporters or the public. It marked a significant watershed moment within the Jehovah's Witnesses organisation, as it was the first time that Watch Tower had allowed private files to be released into the hands of individuals outside of the church. Settling the case also meant that any chance of unsealing the documents remains, for now, unlikely.

The outcome of this case arguably echoes some of the findings of the Royal Commission's 2016 report of 'Case Study No. 29: The Response of the Jehovah's Witnesses and Watchtower Bible and Tract Society of Australia Ltd to Allegations of Child Sexual Abuse', dated October 2016, wherein a synopsis of their findings is presented here:

> Having regard to the various matters we have discussed in this report, we have reached a number of general conclusions on the Jehovah's Witness organisation's response to the sexual abuse of children. We do not consider the Jehovah's Witness organisation to be an organisation which responds adequately to child sexual abuse. We do not believe that children are adequately protected from the risk of sexual abuse for the following reasons:

- The organisation relies on outdated policies and practices to respond to allegations of child sexual abuse. Also, those policies and practices are not subject to ongoing and continuous review. The policies and practices are, by and large, wholly inappropriate and unsuitable for application in cases of child sexual abuse. The organisation's retention and continued application of policies such as the two-witness rule in cases of child sexual abuse shows a serious lack of understanding of the nature of child sexual abuse.

- The organisation's internal disciplinary system for addressing complaints of child sexual abuse is not child or survivor focused in that it is presided over by males and offers a survivor little or no choice about how their complaint is addressed.

- The sanctions available within the organisation's internal disciplinary system are weak and leave perpetrators of child sexual abuse at large in the organisation and the community.

- In deciding the sanctions to impose and/or precautions to take in relation to a known or suspected perpetrator, the organisation has inadequate regard to the risk that that perpetrator might reoffend. This demonstrates a serious lack of understanding of the nature and impact of child sexual abuse.

- The organisation's general practice of not reporting serious instances of child sexual abuse to police or authorities – in particular, where the complainant is a child – demonstrates a serious failure by the organisation to provide for the safety and protection of children in the organisation and in the community.

The Jehovah's Witnesses Church and the Watch Tower Bible and Tract Society responded to the case of Lopez vs Campos as well as the 2016 Royal Commission's report in a consistent message that they 'abhor', and do not sanction, any form of child sex abuse or sex abuse of any nature. The JW.org official website provides a policy document regarding Jehovah's

Witnesses' scripturally based position on child protection. The opening key statements include, but are not limited to, the following:

1. Children are a sacred trust, 'an inheritance from Jehovah'. – Psalm 127:3

2. The protection of children is of utmost concern and importance to all Jehovah's Witnesses. This is in harmony with the long-standing and widely published scripturally based position of Jehovah's Witnesses, as reflected in the references at the end of this document, which are all published on JW.org.

3. Jehovah's Witnesses abhor child abuse and view it as a crime. (Romans 12:9) We recognize that the authorities are responsible for addressing such crimes. (Romans 13:1-4) The elders do not shield any perpetrator of child abuse from the authorities.

4. In all cases, victims and their parents have the right to report an accusation of child abuse to the authorities. Therefore, victims, their parents, or anyone else who reports such an accusation to the elders are clearly informed by the elders that they have the right to report the matter to the authorities. Elders do not criticize anyone who chooses to make such a report. (Galatians 6:5)

Maria's own experience in the Jehovah's Witnesses Church in South Africa is a story of manipulation and despair, but it is also a story of triumph and hope. In leaving the church, Maria was forced to give up her family; she is forbidden to communicate with them and is forever shamed in their eyes.

At the same time, though, she has 'escaped' the many years of torment, confusion and rejection she suffered at the hands of the church. Today, as a former Jehovah's Witness, she stands tall and tells her truth, potentially exposing what lies 'behind closed doors'.

This is her story...

CHAPTER 1

Beginnings

Maria was born in Johannesburg in 1987, and she recalls her earliest years as relatively happy. She was raised in a loving household with a stay-at-home mom and a hard-working, entrepreneurial father who owned several businesses, mostly in the antiques trade. With one sibling and a half-sibling, both older than her, Maria was the baby of the family and the apple of her father's eye. When Maria was eight years old, the family relocated to Cape Town. She says that her father, Albert, was a jovial, charismatic man who was both charming and popular and a devoted husband and father.

Maria's mother, Donna, was the more serious, disciplined partner in the relationship, but a devoted and attentive mother. Donna and Albert were married for nearly thirty-three years before their union would end in divorce, but before then, Maria's early childhood was, overall, happy and stable.

No one in Maria's family had ever been involved with the Jehovah's Witnesses, although her grandmother on Donna's side enjoyed chatting to the occasional Witness who came knocking on her door. She thought it rude not to engage with someone who visited her in the hope of spreading the 'word of God'; they always appeared friendly and courteous, too. She was happy to have their company and would politely offer them a cup of tea, but she certainly wasn't intrigued enough by their conversations to convert to their church.

Donna, on the other hand, was more intrigued by these visits as a teenager, though she only became involved with the Jehovah's Witnesses when she was much older and already married to Albert.

According to Albert, he and Donna never discussed the Jehovah's Witnesses during their courtship. Albert was raised in the Catholic Church, but he later converted to the Anglican faith. However, one of Donna's childhood friends had become a staunch Jehovah's Witness, and it was through her, and the teachings she brought into the family home, that Donna first became drawn to the church.

Shortly after her mother's death, Donna became convinced that it was her mother's dying wish that the whole family convert to the Jehovah's Witnesses faith. And so, after six years of marriage, and soon after Maria's birth, the Jehovah's Witnesses faith took root in the family household, as observed and enforced by Donna.

From the very beginning of their lives, Maria and her older sister, Lara, were raised in a Jehovah's Witnesses home, which grew more orthodox over time. (Maria's eldest sibling, a half-brother from a relationship Albert had had before he married Donna, relocated to Europe with his mother when Maria was still very young.)

Albert was not as convinced by nor as dedicated to the principles of the Jehovah's Witnesses as his wife, but he tolerated Donna's newfound commitment to her faith, though her beliefs would eventually drive them apart and culminate in a divorce many years later.

Albert, though, was a committed Christian in his own way; he was just not swayed by or enamoured with the teachings and prescriptions of the Jehovah's Witnesses faith. He had always enjoyed family celebrations, especially birthdays and Christmases, but Jehovah's Witnesses neither acknowledge nor celebrate these events, which they view as pagan worship or 'Satan's work'.

Although Donna initially tolerated Albert's 'frivolity' when he celebrated these events, as the years passed and her patience wore thin, birthdays and Christmases were gradually phased out of their home.

Maria still remembers how her father had decorated their home at Christmas time, filling stockings with small gifts and placing colourfully wrapped presents beneath a tinsel-laden tree amid much anticipation and excitement. But as Christmas Day drew closer, Donna would make no attempt to hide her disdain. She claimed that Christmas was a pagan tradition and disrespectful of Jehovah. She often got angry and would tell Maria and Lara that after they had opened their presents, they would have to return them or give them away.

On their birthdays, too, any gifts they received from their father or other family members would either be returned or given away. On these occasions, Donna would withdraw from her family and give them the 'silent treatment'. Albert describes how family celebrations became fewer and fewer over the years. Whereas at first it was just Donna who wouldn't take part in the festivities, later Lara also refused to join in. Eventually, Maria was also pressured into boycotting Christmas and birthday celebrations.

On her daughters' birthdays, Donna said that if anyone had to be celebrated, it was her, Donna, in recognition for giving them life. Albert did not want to make a fuss and upset his wife and daughters, so he let the issue slide. However, he felt a deep sadness and anger at the loss of these special occasions. On his own birthday, he says, 'I would just toast myself.'

While losing this childhood ritual did upset Maria, it didn't seem to bother Lara to the same extent. She was in awe of her mother and always wanted to please her. Maria, on the other hand, developed resentment and anger towards Donna, as well as a growing disassociation.

'There was a constant battle waging between me and my mother,' she says, 'particularly on my birthday and at Christmas time.' Albert was also becoming increasingly frustrated with his wife's faith, but not enough for him to draw a firm 'line in the sand'... at least not yet.

He recalls: 'When my wife first got involved with the Jehovah's Witnesses, they seemed like decent people, but as time went on, their presence in our lives became overbearing. Sunday church services took over our weekend time, weekdays were filled with Bible studies, and on Saturdays my wife would take my daughters to do missionary work on the streets in our suburb.

'It was all-consuming, not to mention my favourite time of the year, Christmas, which became a major issue – my wife would just stay upstairs in our bedroom on Christmas morning. I didn't want to rock the boat, but I kept thinking: What is happening to my family?'

Donna was the stricter disciplinarian of the two, while Albert was the more fun and playful parent. Differing as they did in both personality and religion, Maria attributes the longevity of their marriage to the fact that her parents were great friends, and that her father consciously chose not to criticise his wife's principles and beliefs.

For Maria, however, there was only discord in the family set-up. She found it increasingly difficult to remain close to her mother: 'I experienced a passive-aggressive relationship with my mother and an edge of competition with my sister, as she and I seemed to compete for my mother's approval and affection.'

On an emotional level, there was a definitive manipulation of feelings and affection within the household. As the years passed, Maria grew closer to her father and established a stronger connection with him, while her sister, Lara, increasingly enamoured with the Jehovah's Witnesses faith and consumed by a real desire to please her mother, drew closer to Donna, pulling away from Maria and Albert. 'I withdrew from my mom and sister, focusing more on my relationship with my dad. It almost felt like [we were on] two separate teams: my mom and my sister versus Dad and me.'

Lara had raised a symbolic but definite barrier between her and Maria – if Maria didn't genuinely show that she was embracing the Witness faith, Lara shut her out. Maria explains how her resentment towards Donna and Lara escalated over time: 'I felt outside of their bubble. My sister was the golden girl and followed "the Truth", while I always resisted to conform. I felt like an outsider. Mom always said God was rewarding my sister for following Jehovah and the Truth.'

The JW.org website explains that '"The Truth" refers to Jehovah's Witnesses' adherence to the form of Christianity that Jesus taught and that His apostles practised – learning, teaching, and living this "truth" as Jesus once spoke and practised is the cornerstone of their existence: "O Jehovah ... the very essence of your word is Truth." – Psalm 119:159, 160.'

Maria recalls the Jehovah's Witnesses' mantra by which she was raised and that her mother constantly asked her to abide by: 'Put Jehovah first and all other things will be given to you.' Furthermore, as Jehovah's Witnesses are required to minimise social contact with non–Jehovah's Witnesses, otherwise referred to as 'worldly people', Maria found this aspect of her religious upbringing not only challenging but completely isolating during her school years.

As controversial activist and former Jehovah's Witness Lloyd Evans writes in his book *The Reluctant Apostate*, if you are one of the 99.9% of earth's population who is not a Witness, 'then you are one of those cursed people – a "worldly" person'. The term 'worldly' implies a wicked, tainted individual, part of Satan's influence on earth. 'It is irrelevant whether you are religious or atheist, Christian or Buddhist,' Evans writes. 'You could be a doctor or fireman, someone who works in a soup kitchen, or someone who helps old ladies across the street and rescues stray kittens. It doesn't matter. You are still worldly, in a "spiritually destitute condition", and therefore deemed a corrupting influence – unsuitable material for friendship or association.'

The Jehovah's Witnesses website responds to the perils of 'worldly people' by politely explaining their 'relationship towards others': 'Jesus commanded: "You must love your neighbour as yourself." He also said that Christians "are no part of the world". (Matthew 22:39; John 17:16) So we try to "work what is good toward all", yet we remain strictly neutral in political affairs and avoid affiliation with other religions. (Galatians 6:10; 2 Corinthians 6:14) However, we respect the choices that others make in such matters. (Romans 14:12).'

Although, outwardly, this official stance of Jehovah's Witnesses towards non–Jehovah's Witnesses appears neutral, there is arguably a subliminal call to either shun or convert them – there is no middle ground. Socialising with 'worldly' non-Witnesses is not acceptable, which Maria's school experiences can attest to. During her primary-school years, Maria met and socialised with other Jehovah's Witnesses who attended her local community school, which was a public school open to everyone in the area. It just happened to have a generous number of students who were Jehovah's Witnesses.

While there was some comfort in this familiarity, the rest of the school stigmatised Maria and the other Witnesses, which was a huge embarrassment for her. As a Witness, she was not allowed to attend school assemblies during which school songs, religious hymns or the national anthem were sung. These are considered symbols of Satan's influence on earth.

So, during school assemblies, Maria and her Witness friends either abstained from attending or had to excuse themselves in front of the entire school when it was time to sing a hymn or the anthem: 'The Witness children had to first stand and be led out of the assembly. This resulted in constant embarrassment as well as teasing and bullying,' she says.

Maria recalls the elders in her congregation explaining that the Jehovah's Witnesses faith was the only true religion, that it practised and taught the absolute 'Truth', as Jesus intended, and anything else taught in any other religion is not 'the Truth'. This was the reason why Maria and her Witness friends could not participate in school assemblies or sing the hymns.

Even at her young age, Maria felt as if this was a form of brainwashing, and it left her confused. Feeling both guilty and ashamed of questioning her faith, she was also completely embarrassed by it, as she was forced to practise her faith so publicly. And she was angry at the constant teasing and bullying meted out by her peers: 'I hated every single minute of my school life.'

On one occasion, Maria joined in to celebrate a friend's birthday at their primary school. This friend was not a Jehovah's Witness: 'She was one of my best friends and I wanted her to feel special on her birthday. I also wanted to be part of the celebration and not always [feel like] the stick in the mud.'

Her participation was short-lived. Elders from the local Jehovah's Witnesses congregation (the Kingdom Hall, as they are known) were informed of Maria's 'wandering' behaviour and took it upon themselves to visit her and Donna at home that same day, demanding that Maria's 'paganistic' behaviour stop immediately. She says: 'I think a fellow Jehovah's Witness at the school, maybe a teacher or another student, felt it their right to tell on me.'

She was duly punished for her involvement in the birthday celebration, though she can't remember exactly what the punishment entailed. Quite likely, it involved withholding from her something that was fun or pleasant, such as an outing to the beach or playtime with friends.

In addition to school assemblies and birthday celebrations, Maria explains that Witness children are discouraged from participating in any competitive sport. Extramural activities and sport are for the purposes of health and fitness only, which put paid to any aspirations Maria might have had to join the school swimming or netball team. In his book, *I, Witness*, Daniel Clark, a former Witness, describes his disappointment at not being allowed to celebrate birthdays or Christmases, and, more significantly, not being allowed to partake in extracurricular activities at school or to compete in sport:

> I discovered this the hard way in high school when I inadvertently tested the boundaries of my parents' dedication to Watchtower doctrine. I tried out for and was accepted into my high school wrestling and cross-

> country teams. I can't begin to describe what this meant to me: To earn a 'letter' for a sport, to win awards for my abilities, to be somebody among my peers ... to make my father proud of me. It was with this thrilling prospect filling my head and heart that I arrived home one afternoon with a duffel bag full of my school-issued sports gear and a list of things my parents needed to buy.

Sadly, for this young man, his father was anything but proud. Instead, he was livid, ordering his son to 'Take it back! Take the equipment back! You're not going to do sports.' Confused and hurt by his father's reaction, Clark was told that competing in school sports was a 'dangerous' pastime, as it would require him to train and possibly socialise with non-Witness children. His father explained that this would be 'an unwholesome association to "worldly youths" – the only time one should associate with them is when trying to convert them'.

In any event, there was no time for extramural activities or sport for Maria, as most afternoons were taken up with Bible-study sessions. Every day after school, an hour was set aside for personal Bible study and the reading of the Daily Scriptures of Jehovah. This, over and above her normal homework for school. While Lara enjoyed Bible study, Maria suffered this daily duty. Then there were also the two hours of communal Bible study every Tuesday evening at their local Kingdom Hall, plus a further two hours of missionary training every Thursday evening where, from a pre-school age, Witnesses were taught how to approach and engage with non–Jehovah's Witnesses to spread 'the Truth'.

Weekends were devoted to more personal Bible-study time, ministry service and, of course, church attendance on Sundays. It was all-consuming and overwhelming. Dan Clark reveals a similar experience to Maria's in *I, Witness*, where, even as an adult and with his own family, he continued with the relentless cycle of missionary work and Bible study:

> I made sure my family participated in all five weekly meetings – an exhausting schedule of book study, theocratic ministry school, meetings for field service, public talk, and Watchtower meetings. We went door-to-door on Saturdays. I do not exaggerate when I use the word

> 'exhausting.' I have seen women go from vibrant and vital to limp and worn out trying to keep family and service apace. I've watched men – like my father – have the spring leached out of their step with every year as they tried to balance work and worship. And the children? One would think that considering how hard I'd found the meetings as a boy, I'd have some empathy with my own children. I didn't. Strong discipline is highly regarded at meetings in the Kingdom Hall, and it is a credit to any parent whose kids can sit still for two hours at a time.

Door-to-door preaching is a fundamental and compulsory ministerial activity that all Witnesses must perform, even the elderly. A minimum of fifteen minutes a month is set aside for this purpose. Truly incapacitated and frail Witnesses may seek exemption from their local elders. In *The Reluctant Apostate*, Evans explains that when a Witness calls at your home, one should not assume that they are there without having been coerced or feeling obligated: 'While it is true that Witnesses do not earn a salary for their evangelical work, it cannot honestly be said that they are under no pressure to engage in it.'

Witnesses are generally required to keep a careful count of the exact number of hours they spend on people's doorsteps and the amount of time spent preaching. 'These "field service" hours are almost a form of currency among believers,' Evans writes. 'The more hours a Witness writes down, the more spiritually oriented he or she must be. The more hours you are able to report, the more you are "storing up treasures in heaven".'

Local elders may review the number of hours that are spent spreading 'the Truth' every month so that they can determine if there are any 'spiritually weak' Witnesses in the congregation who need a 'shepherding visit' – 'a visit from elders that is generally used either to offer encouragement or warn against errant behaviour', writes Evans. Also recorded in one's field-service hours is the number of Bible-study groups that one has conducted, and/or the number of educational materials or 'placements' that have been left behind after each house visit, which can include pamphlets, magazines, books, any digital information sent via email and, of course, any return visits.

According to Evans, every Witness is encouraged from a young age to enlist as a 'pioneer', which could best be described as an 'über-Witness'.

A pioneer commits to spending at least seventy hours per month on the duty of preaching. In addition to the term 'pioneer', Jehovah's Witnesses also use the term 'publisher' to refer to anyone who is an active participant in organised preaching activity, as in Witnesses who 'publish' the word of Jehovah in active preaching (but not necessarily to the same amount of time as a pioneer).

Active publishers who preach 'The Truth' of Jehovah are officially counted as fully fledged members of the Jehovah's Witnesses Church. Publishers can be baptised or unbaptised, but if they are not yet baptised and want to become an unbaptised publisher, they would demonstrate their commitment by regularly attending Bible studies and congregation meetings, sharing their learnings with others, loving Jehovah and choosing as close friends those who also love Him, and, most importantly, withdrawing all membership from political or 'false' religious associations.

An unbaptised publisher may decide to get baptised if they are already considered an unbaptised publisher, they participate in as much preaching work as possible, and have decided to dedicate themself to Jehovah in prayer and want to serve Him forever.

As with ordinary publishers, pioneers receive no payment for their efforts and are expected to meet their financial needs by way of part-time employment, or support from their parents and family. Their reward? The admiration and recognition of their congregation, not to mention a clear conscience.

If a pioneer fails to fulfil their pledge of seventy hours a month during the course of a year, whether due to illness or financial issues, the respect and reverence they enjoyed up till then may be swiftly replaced with disapproval, or even a shameful removal of their 'pioneer' title. 'There are no prizes for almost succeeding,' writes Evans in *The Reluctant Apostate*.

Teenagers, especially, find themselves under immense pressure to pioneer once they finish school, not only to please their congregation but, mostly, to please their parents. Maria started learning how to conduct home visits and engage in door-to-door preaching from the age of four, when she was shown children's Bible-study books that illustrated door-to-door preaching and the call to ministerial service in the name of Jehovah.

Albert says that it was the door-to-door missionary work that eventually led him to draw 'the line in the sand' – it became the source of numerous heated arguments with his wife: 'They would take my kids and use them to knock on people's doors and push the word of God. I had a big issue with this. Not only were my kids very young, but my opinion as a father was also never taken into consideration. I argued with [Donna] to let Maria stay at home because she was still so young, but [Lara] appeared to enjoy it and really bought into the whole idea of door-to-door missionary work. I sensed she was pulling away from me. I didn't want to lose her, so I let it be.

'Now, when I think about it all, I become so angry and frustrated that I didn't do more. I really believe the Jehovah's Witnesses Church was instrumental in the break-up of my family.'

Another of Maria's earliest recollections of the Witness church was her struggle to concentrate on and find meaning in the weekly church services that she, Donna and Lara were compelled to attend. Maria was gifted with a natural artistic talent, and she loved to draw, paint and colour in her art books. To stave off her boredom, she would often take her colouring-in books and crayons to church with her. Donna, though, told Maria to rather use the time to record interesting biblical names or terms and write them down in her book. If she didn't do this, she would be punished.

Of course, every Sunday, while the church service was taking place, Maria was hell-bent on colouring in her favourite pictures, deliberately disobeying her mother's instructions and oblivious to the teachings of the elders. Donna would look warningly in Maria's direction and mouth the words, 'Just wait till we get home!' Sometimes, she would even pinch Maria under her arms to get her to stop drawing. Despite dreading the punishment that awaited her, Maria remained defiant. On their return home, Maria would face the wrath of her mother, usually by way of a slap on the bottom with a wet slipper.

Maria soon found new and ingenious ways of escaping punishment by either hiding from her mother or padding her underwear with sponges to soften the blow from that ever-ready slipper, which further enraged Donna. Maria never relented or gave in to her mother's demands. She was bold and high-spirited from the start, setting her apart from her obliging sister and driving the wedge between her and Donna deeper with each passing year.

Despite Maria's resentment and anger towards Donna's strictness and the many admonishments she endured for being a 'worldly' and 'unspiritual' Witness, she genuinely does try to understand why Donna was, and still is today, so unconditionally devoted to the Jehovah's Witnesses despite the emotional cost to her and her family.

According to Maria, by comparison, Donna had a difficult childhood, navigating the challenges of divorce from a young age. Seeking solace from some of these challenges, Donna was drawn to God and Christianity at an early age, and when the Jehovah's Witnesses came 'knocking at her door' and presented the ultimate in 'purist salvation', she found her deliverance. The Jehovah's Witnesses offered her both the comfort and the structure she craved.

While the foundations of the Jehovah's Witnesses Church rocked Donna's world, it did nothing for Maria. Ultimately, it would destroy her parents' marriage and fuel the disintegration of her family. The controlling and unyielding nature of the Witness lifestyle would become too suffocating, eventually driving Albert away. By 2004, he had started a relationship with another woman, marking the beginning of the end of his and Donna's marriage.

Up until that point, Maria believes her father had been tolerant of Donna's life choices and her commitment to her faith. He had done his best to accept, and even socialise with her many Witness friends and associates: 'Dad was considered the "goat" by many of mom's Witness friends, and they considered themselves the sheep, always trying to influence him, using subtle bullying tactics in an attempt to convert him.'

Despite the fact that Albert attended a few Bible meetings and tried to socialise with the Witness community, he was never interested in converting or being baptised into the faith. Instead, he preferred to remain 'neutral'. His priority was to keep his family together and, for that reason, he tolerated as much as he could for as long as possible. Ultimately, though, the church and its draconian, demanding methods became too much to bear, he says. Members were discouraged from thinking for themselves and he could no longer take it: 'They seem to behave like a cult,' he explains.

Maria, too, spent much of her youth physically present but emotionally and spiritually detached from the Jehovah's Witnesses' fold. She tried to oblige her mother but remained mentally and spiritually disengaged from the church and all that it represented. As she grew older, her attitude became more defiant. She rebelled against the church's rules and regulations, was confused by its teachings and embarrassed by its restrictions.

Maria explains how the weight of the Jehovah's Witnesses' presence in their home became unbearable: 'I always felt uneasy, inadequate and unconvinced by it all. Mostly, however, I felt trapped – caged like an animal – because our lives were controlled by this religion that was so restrictive. I couldn't be myself; I couldn't make real friends; every day was pre-planned according to how the Witnesses said we should live. I never felt free. I always felt like someone was watching me.'

Maria felt stifled: she wasn't allowed to wear the clothes she liked or cut her hair into a 'funky' style, or even laugh too loudly. 'It was a bland and boring life. If I wore a skirt that wasn't long enough or a top that had skimpy straps or if I showed any kind of cleavage, I was pulled aside and told that I was projecting evil thoughts and distracting the elders.'

CHAPTER 2

'Knock Knock' Who's There?

'We come from hundreds of ethnic and language backgrounds, yet we are united by common goals. Above all, we want to honour Jehovah, the God of the Bible and the Creator of all things. We do our best to imitate Jesus Christ and are proud to be called Christians. Each of us regularly spends time helping people learn about the Bible and God's Kingdom. Because we witness, or talk, about Jehovah God and his Kingdom, we are known as Jehovah's Witnesses.' – JW.org

ORIGINS OF THE JEHOVAH'S WITNESSES

The Jehovah's Witnesses Church is a worldwide, Christian-based organisation with a global reach of over 8 million members. They worship the one, true Almighty God, whom they call Jehovah. Their beliefs are based on all sixty-six books of the Bible, in both the Old and New Testaments.

The Jehovah's Witnesses originally began as an Adventist movement in the early nineteenth century, eventually emerging as a branch of Protestant Christianity that focuses on the Second Coming, or Second Advent, of Jesus Christ. Its first proponent, Baptist preacher William Miller, founder of the religious movement known as Millerism, predicted that the Second Coming was imminent and would occur at some point between 1843 and 1844.

Miller was particularly drawn to the Book of Daniel and based his predictions on his interpretation of Daniel 8:14, which spoke of 2300 days. Miller claimed that it meant the return of Jesus Christ would occur in 1843. He began preaching his predictions in 1831, essentially launching the Adventist movement with his followers, known as Millerites.

When Jesus did not appear on this date, however, Miller acknowledged a mathematical error in his calculations and claimed that Jesus would, in fact, return the following year, in March 1844, and then actually only in

October 1844. When Jesus again failed to appear on either of these dates, Miller's followers grew wary and splintered off into separate sects, each with their own beliefs and doctrines, one of which became the Seventh-day Adventists, which is still active today.

Miller's following dwindled to just a handful of people and even smaller groupings of separatist Adventists. One such group, led by writer and publisher Nelson H. Barbour, claimed that Jesus did, in fact, return in 1847, but had done so invisibly. Barbour went on to sow the seeds of the prophecy of Armageddon, claiming that Jehovah would save and resurrect some faithful devotees to an earthly paradise when the world ended in 1848. The big prize, however, was reserved for an elite few (exactly 144 000) who would be resurrected and taken to live in heaven with Jehovah.

Barbour's publications captured the attention of another Christian minister, Charles Taze Russell, of Pittsburgh, Pennsylvania, who, today, is regarded as the official founder of the Jehovah's Witnesses. Russell initially partnered with Barbour to expedite further publications, and, with Russell's funding, their publications grew exponentially, as did their readership base.

Their partnership, on the other hand, did not last. Russell and Barbour eventually parted ways, with Russell forming his own group of Bible Students in 1872. Based in Pennsylvania, this movement was formally established in 1884 and became known as the Watch Tower Bible and Tract Society, cited as the original legal entity of what is today the Jehovah's Witnesses Church. According to JW.org:

> Besides the Watch Tower Bible and Tract Society of Pennsylvania, Jehovah's Witnesses use dozens of legal entities in various countries. Some of these entities include in their name such terms as 'Watch Tower', 'Watchtower', or a translation of one of these. These various legal entities have enabled us to accomplish much since they were established, including printing and publishing, education, and charitable endeavours.

Under Russell's leadership, the Bible Students occupied themselves with analysing and interpreting the Bible. Comparing what was preached in various churches with what the Bible taught – or at least what they believed it taught – Russell's Bible Students began publishing their own interpretations of the Good Book in various journals and newspapers via Russell's own in-house printing and publishing operations. This culminated in the first edition of *The Watchtower* (a journal/magazine still produced today) in 1879, with its sole purpose to announce the Kingdom of Jehovah.

Lloyd Evans claims that Russell's popularity could be ascribed to being in the right place at the right time: 'Russell allowed himself to be swept along on a tide of late 19th century evangelical hysteria at a time when almost anyone with a bit of money and charisma – and preferably an unconventional take on the Bible – would probably have had little difficulty attracting an audience.'

In 1881, Bible Student missionaries were sent to England to spread the word of Jehovah. In 1900, the first overseas branch of Jehovah's Witnesses was opened, in London. By 1909, Russell had moved his headquarters to Brooklyn, New York, where it remained for over a hundred years, before relocating to the town of Warwick, Orange County, New York State, in 2015.

Russell's plan had been to purchase a substantial property that could house both their corporate offices and printing operations, as well as a house of worship. Volunteers would reside in a nearby property referred to as Bethel. A 2015 *Mail Online* article states that 'Over the next hundred years, the group amassed 36 buildings scattered across Brooklyn.'

What is most significant was Russell's ability to oversee and retain the publishing activities of all Jehovah's Witnesses' publications, magazines and Bible books as an in-house operation, independent of public peer review or scrutiny, and autonomous of mainstream publishers who would likely have applied more rigour and asked more questions during the editing process.

To this day, all Jehovah's Witnesses' literature is printed in-house and distributed by each congregation worldwide. This exclusive control over the publishing of their reading material has raised the question of credibility in Jehovah's Witnesses' publications, and, arguably, throws their educational material under the moniker of 'fake news'.

The Watch Tower Bible and Tract Society of Pennsylvania continues to publish their own translation of the Bible, known as *The New World Translation of the Holy Scriptures*, originally published in 1961 as a complete version that included both the Old and New Testaments (it was most recently revised in 2013). It is now also available online via different book-ordering sites as well as through the JW.org official website. This translation of the Bible has been published in whole, or in part, in over 210 languages worldwide, according to JW.org.

As the Jehovah's Witnesses network spread outside of the United States, to the United Kingdom, Europe, Africa and beyond, new Bethels were built in the towns and countries where Jehovah's Witnesses found a foothold. Bethel – Hebrew for the 'House of God' – refers to the local headquarters in various geographical locations where Jehovah's Witnesses come together to live and work, to serve God, to co-ordinate their preaching activities and to provide leadership to their local communities.

As the JW.org website states: 'Bethel is a fitting designation for the complexes that Jehovah's Witnesses have established around the world from which the preaching work is directed and supported. The Governing Body serves at the world headquarters in New York State, U.S.A., and from there it supervises the activity of the branch offices in scores of countries.'

At every Bethel, men and women who are devoted to doing Jehovah's work, and to serving Kingdom interests full-time, come together as one 'Bethel family' – or Bethelites, as they are known. They do not receive a wage or income but are provided with room and board and an allowance to assist with personal expenses. Each person is given individual responsibilities, either serving in an administrative capacity or overseeing general maintenance, or working in the printing operations, kitchen, dining area or laundry. JW.org describes it as 'a busy place that supports Kingdom preaching. The main objective of every Bethel is to make Bible truth available to as many people as possible.'

Perhaps the most impressive of the Bethels is the newly built facility at the Jehovah's Witnesses' global headquarters in Warwick, upstate New York, a 102-hectare property with a state-of-the-art, 18-hectare, purpose-built facility that includes offices and four residences, all surrounded by untouched forests and wetlands. Apart from the printing complex in Wallkill, New York, Jehovah's Witnesses also have an educational centre in Patterson, New York. Visitors are welcome at all their global facilities and are invited to take a tour and meet their Bethel families. (The Jehovah's Witnesses' Bethel headquarters in South Africa is situated in the mining town of Krugersdorp, on the West Rand of Gauteng.)

Russell and his following of Witnesses continued to preach their interpretation of the Bible and perform their duties in the name of the Kingdom of Jehovah with a growing emphasis on Jehovah's plan to eradicate the world of all 'worldly' people, who were influenced by and integral to Satan's system on earth. In his preachings, Russell also denied the existence of hell, as well as that of the Holy Trinity.

Unlike other Christian-based faiths, Jehovah's Witnesses believe that only the Father, Jehovah, is God, and that his son, Jesus, is a separate living entity. The Holy Spirit exists only as a force, rather than as part of a living Trinity. Perhaps the most significant of his preachings, however, was Russell's claim that Jesus, God's only son, would return in 1914 with the commencement of Armageddon. Notably, the only global event to take place that year was the start of World War 1.

After Russell's death in 1916, Joseph Franklin Rutherford became the second president of the Watch Tower Bible and Tract Society in 1917, a position he retained until his death in 1942. During his twenty-five-year reign, more than twenty Watchtower books were published. It was during Rutherford's tenure, in 1931, that the Bible Students changed their name to Jehovah's Witnesses.

Nathan H. Knorr took over from Rutherford in 1942, again claiming that the end of the world was near. Knorr was succeeded by Frederick Franz in 1977 until his death in 1992, after which Milton Henschel took the lead. He died in 2003. According to an online Catholic publication, *Catholic Answers*, the Jehovah's Witnesses underwent a fundamental doctrine shift during the mid-nineties: 'In 1995, The Watchtower [Society] quietly changed one of its major prophetic doctrines. Until this point, they had maintained that the generation alive in 1914 would not pass from the scene until Armageddon occurred. Now that this generation has almost entirely died out, they had to change their doctrine. Now, the Watchtower says that Armageddon will simply occur "soon," and is no longer tied to a particular, literal generation of people.'

According to former Witness Daniel Clark: 'The November 1995 issue of *Watchtower* said of Jesus' prophecy about "this generation" that it "apparently refers to the peoples of earth (now) who see the signs of Christ's presence but fail to mend their ways". The Great Clock had stopped ticking. After 130 plus years of urgent preaching about the impending end of the world, the Watchtower Society had reinterpreted the prophecy in such a way that there was no end in sight.'

For a devout Witness, this was potentially devastating: an 'infallible' prophecy by which they had faithfully lived their entire lives had suddenly just changed! For someone who had lived their life with the belief that 'the end was near', this change in doctrine was potentially life-shattering. As Clark writes in *I, Witness*, Witness children forego pleasures that other children take for granted, education is not necessarily a priority, competitive sport is considered an evil pastime and any association with non-Witnesses is actively discouraged. In fact, non-Witnesses are viewed as evil influences, sinful in their actions and forever doomed:

> As a teen, you reject an advanced education and career training because to do so would be a futile waste of time. As an adult you may forego having a family, a career or even a full-time job because time is so short that all your energy must go toward pioneering.

As a result of his beliefs, Clark approached adulthood with no real-life skills or practical capabilities. He had a poor education and no future direction other than to anticipate the end of the world. 'It was the ultimate irony: in my youth I had been without purpose because I had strayed from the beliefs that had defined my life to that point. As an adult, I found myself in the same position because those beliefs had been redefined.' He was prepared for the end of the world but totally unprepared for the world he lived in.

Today, Jehovah's Witnesses, known collectively around the world as the Watch Tower Society, are organised and led by their Governing Body, a group of all-male, long-serving senior Witnesses who are based at the Watch Tower Society's headquarters in Warwick, New York. JW.org says that while the size of the Governing Body may vary between six and twelve members at any given time, its main role is to provide direction to all Jehovah's Witnesses worldwide, including all operational responsibilities of the global ministry, oversight of Bible-based education, co-ordination of the publishing and distribution of instructional materials, and the oversight of the use of donated funds.

Of course, Jehovah's Witnesses regard Jehovah God as their one true leader, with the Governing Body merely standing in as His representative, destined to follow and implement His 'Truth' on earth. 'The members of the Governing Body are not the leaders of our organization. They look to the Bible for guidance, acknowledging that Jehovah God has appointed Jesus Christ as the Head of the congregation,' claims JW.org.

JEHOVAH'S WITNESSES WORLDWIDE

Fast Facts

The following 2023 statistics and fast facts about Jehovah's Witnesses have been sourced from their official website, JW.org:

- 239 – Countries and islands where Jehovah's Witnesses worship
- 8 686 980 – Worldwide population of Jehovah's Witnesses
- 5 908 167 – Free home Bible courses conducted worldwide
- 119 297 – Congregations

JEHOVAH'S WITNESSES IN SOUTH AFRICA

Fast Facts

The following facts about Jehovah's Witnesses in South Africa have been sourced from their official website as of 2022:

- 60 605 000 – Population of South Africa
- 97 639 – Publishers
- 1999 – Congregations
- 1 to 629 – Ratio of 1 publisher to population
- 96 385 – Average number of publishers in 2022
- 1953 – Number of newly baptised Witnesses in 2022
- 1902 – The year Jehovah's Witnesses was first established in South Africa
- 188 000 – Printed magazines per hour, distributing literature to almost twenty African countries

HISTORICAL FOOTPRINT IN SOUTH AFRICA

The first Bible Study publications by a Dutch missionary arrived in South Africa in 1902. Two local clergymen, Frans Ebersohn and Stoffel Fourie, both from Klerksdorp, took what they read as 'the Truth' and began witnessing to others, according to JW.org. More than eighty relatives of the Fourie family, spanning five generations, and several descendants of the Ebersohn family, became dedicated servants of Jehovah.

Thus, the Jehovah's Witnesses in South Africa was established. Its local development has not been without its challenges, however, particularly during the apartheid era, when Kingdom Halls were prohibited from being built in non-white areas and mixed-race congregations were illegal. Then there was also the challenge of compulsory military conscription during the late 1960s, '70s and '80s.

Throughout these decades, Witness brothers conscientiously objected to serving in South Africa's Defence Force and fighting in South Africa's Border War with Angola. Instead of doing their military service, Witnesses were often imprisoned, stigmatised and forced into lengthy hours of government-sanctioned community service. Stoic and committed as ever, viewing any challenge to their faith as a test of their conviction, the Jehovah's Witnesses navigated these years without equivocation.

In 1999, Jehovah's Witnesses arranged for Kingdom Halls to be built on the African continent in countries with limited resources. A regional Kingdom Hall office was established in South Africa to co-ordinate the purchasing of land and all construction work across several African countries. Witnesses from overseas were also sent to volunteer their support and train their local brothers. The South African regional office established twenty-five Kingdom Hall Construction Desks in Africa, which catered for Kingdom Hall construction in thirty-seven countries.

Since November 1999, more than 7 207 Kingdom Halls have been built in countries served by this arrangement. The work of Jehovah's Witnesses is also well entrenched within the borders of South Africa's closest neighbours, like Namibia, Botswana, Lesotho and Swaziland. There is even an established network on the island of St Helena, according to JW.org: 'The island has a Publisher-to-population ratio of 1 to 30, the most favourable in the world.'

The Jehovah's Witnesses Church in South Africa prides itself on its capacity to publish widely across various languages by way of over a hundred translators and produces Witness literature in all thirteen official languages. It is also active in the deaf community, using South African Sign Language (SASL) to conduct one-on-one Bible discussions, local congregation meetings and larger gatherings. Sign-language publications are also available electronically (on DVD) at local Kingdom Halls.

While missionary work within the deaf community is voluntary and publications are distributed at no charge, financial contributions are always welcome. As of December 2009, church sermons and teachings are 'signed' directly by the lead speaker in various congregations located in Bloemfontein, Gauteng, Cape Town, Durban, George, West Rand (Randfontein), Soweto, East Rand (Kempton Park) and Tshwane.

BEHIND THE GATES OF JEHOVAH'S KINGDOM

Core Belief System

Jehovah's Witnesses preach about love and acceptance across all races and ethnicities. They strive to show unselfish love and avoid all practices that might displease Jehovah, including the misuse of blood by taking blood transfusions, celebrating pagan holidays such as Christmas, and celebrating birthdays and material gifting on one's birthday. They abstain from warfare and remain politically neutral, and they avoid affiliation with other religions, yet they claim to respect the choices that others make in their own lives.

Worship

Jehovah's Witnesses do not worship the cross or any other image. They view these as idol worship. From the scriptures in the Bible, they interpret that Jesus did not die on a cross, but rather a 'simple wooden stake', as quoted on JW.org.

Wearing a crucifix or cross as jewellery is strictly forbidden. Their focus is squarely on praying to Jehovah, studying the Bible, and meeting together to pray and experience the Bible and to express their faith. Preaching the 'good news' of the Kingdom to others is fundamental to their cause, as is building and maintaining their places of worship (Kingdom Halls) and other facilities around the world for their Bible-education work.

Jehovah's Witnesses' beliefs are based on their interpretation of the scriptures and teachings in the Bible and are collectively referred to as 'the Truth'. Unfortunately, though, in Anthony James's book, *'Knock Knock' Who's There? 'The Truth' About Jehovah's Witnesses*, he claims that, over the years, this 'Truth' has changed many times on multiple key doctrines, often to accommodate worldwide socio-political changes or just to explain away the non-event of Armageddon: 'If "the Truth" has had to change, it clearly wasn't always the truth. Yet followers were expected to obey and believe false things, until they were later "corrected".'

THE KINGDOM OF GOD

Jehovah's Witnesses follow the teachings and example of Jesus Christ and honour him as their Saviour and as the Son of Jehovah God, but, in their view, Jesus is not Almighty God and there is no scriptural basis for the Trinity doctrine. The Kingdom of Jehovah God is a real government in heaven, not a condition in the hearts of Christians, and it will replace human governments after the 'final days' on earth, claims JW.org.

To benefit from these 'final days' and the associated trauma of experiencing and surviving an event as cataclysmic as Armageddon, people must not only have faith in Jehovah but also change their course of life and get baptised.

According to JW.org, evil and suffering were brought upon the earth when one of Jehovah's angels rebelled. Known as Satan, he persuaded the first human couple to join his cause, the consequences of which have affected their descendants ever since. 'In order to settle the moral issues raised by Satan, God has allowed evil and suffering, but He will not permit them to continue forever.'

JW.org further claims that people do not die – rather, they pass out of existence. There is no hell. After the 'final days' of Armageddon, Jehovah will bring billions back from death by means of a resurrection, but those who refuse to repent or learn his ways after being resurrected will be destroyed forever. As Evans writes in *The Reluctant Apostate*:

> Despite the teaching of a future earthly paradise being based on extremely tenuous foundations, it is a hope that forms the basic incentive for millions of Witnesses to radically set themselves apart from the world around them. It is what drives Witnesses to call at your door in all weather. It is what impels Witness parents to shun their wayward teenagers. It is what moves Witness parents to allow their children to die for want of a blood transfusion.

The prophecy of Armageddon and the promise of a utopian afterlife, where all Witnesses, except for the elite core of 144 000, will be rewarded for their loyal service with eternal life in an earthly paradise, begs this question: What will happen to the billions of bodies left behind after the annihilation of humankind?

Evans asks the following questions in *The Reluctant Apostate*: 'With 8 billion humans and only 8 million Jehovah's Witnesses, who will bury the dead and cleanse the earth of the human death toll? Will birds like ravens and vultures and other carrion birds do this job by themselves, or will they complement the work of the many grave diggers that will come from the survivors and who would likely spend a lifetime digging graves?'

The Governing Body of the Jehovah's Witnesses appears not to want to comment, and their official website does not provide practical answers to the questions that surround Armageddon. In Rachel Walsh's book, *The Day of Jehovah's Witnesses*, she claims that only through extreme indoctrination and a steadfast belief that everyone who is not a Witness is 'wicked and deserving of death' can there be a plausible explanation for this 'placid contemplation of such bloodletting'.

Interestingly, in reference to the 'chosen' 144 000 Witnesses who will take their rightful place in heaven, Maria recalls that, on some occasions, members of her congregation spontaneously stood up and declared that they had had a vision telling them that they had been chosen. To be one of the 144 000 is a 'divine' calling, and only the most righteous and devout of Witnesses can claim that they are without sin, that they are among the purest in their congregation and thus eligible to be chosen by Jehovah.

When they 'experience' this self-professed 'calling', they may stand up in Kingdom Hall and announce it. Once they have done so, no one seems to question their declaration; the individual is unconditionally 'anointed'. This begs another question: Over the decades, just how many of the 144 000 'seats' in heaven have been claimed by the self-proclaimed, and is heaven not already vastly oversubscribed?

THE 'GO BAG'

In preparation for Armageddon, all Witness families are reportedly required to be 'disaster ready' by way of a disaster-relief kit, their so-called 'go bag'. At church meetings, witnesses are regularly reminded to stock and restock all essential tinned foods, clothing, medicine and equipment in preparation for the 'final days' and informed of where the rendezvous points are when they are called to gather for Armageddon.

A Witness of Jehovah must not be caught unprepared when Jehovah says it is time. Jehovah will know where his Witnesses are, and he will protect them. In the Bible's Book of Daniel, which is widely read and respected by Jehovah's Witnesses, Daniel's prophecies describe the events at the end of the world and how a new world order and a new paradise on earth will come into being. The 'end' will be marked by an increasing number of earthquakes and natural disasters, famine and disease. When the Covid-19 pandemic erupted globally in 2019, many Jehovah's Witnesses believed that this was the beginning of the end. Maria recalls that at Kingdom Hall meetings, Witnesses were told to go home and pack their 'go bags', and to be ready.

Interestingly, in July 2023, the homepage for the JW.org website displayed an ominous image of planet earth being consumed in a ball of flames with the heading: 'Keep on the Watch! Summer 2023 Global Heat Wave – What Does the Bible Say?' It went on to quote alarming statistics about humans having to endure global, record-breaking heatwaves and extreme weather events. The text followed with the most pressing question of all: 'Do these extreme conditions fulfil Bible prophecy?' The answer was a resounding 'Yes!'

However, the article was not referring to an impending Armageddon, but rather to the rationale that climate change is a sign that all earthly ways of life are about to change – a change that will soon be brought about by the Kingdom of Jehovah God. Earth will be restored, and the Kingdom of Heaven will then rule upon it, destroying and superseding all earthly, human governments.

For faithful Witnesses, rising global temperatures should not be a cause for concern because Jehovah God will prevent total environmental disaster in order to fulfil the promise of eternal salvation on a newly restored, healthy planet. Jehovah God will ensure that the planet remains an everlasting home for Jehovah's Witnesses, and the heavenly government, under the leadership of Jesus Christ, will administer earth's affairs.

No date was mentioned for this momentous event, but it was implied that it could happen soon. 'You can expect that God's Kingdom will soon bring about these changes. God will replace human governments, which have been unable to protect the earth, with a perfect heavenly Kingdom (Daniel 2:44; Matthew 6:9, 10). That Kingdom will be ruled by God's Son, Jesus Christ (Isaiah 9:6, 7).'

ORGANISATIONAL STRUCTURE

From the humble beginnings in 1884 of the Watch Tower Bible and Tract Society of Pennsylvania, with its many subsequent affiliated legal entities, often collectively referred to as Watchtower, the Jehovah's Witnesses Church has grown into an 8-million-strong global network. They are organised into congregations of about a hundred believers, each overseen by a body of spiritually mature men known as elders, who are not paid a salary, and no tithing is accepted.

All baptised Witnesses are ordained ministers and share in the preaching and teaching work. The worldwide church is overseen by a Governing Body of mature Christians who serve at their world headquarters in New York, providing overall strategic direction for Jehovah's Witnesses around the world.

The worldwide congregation of Jehovah's Witnesses comprises individuals ready to follow and observe the ways of Jehovah. Jehovah's Witnesses who are active participants in preaching the word of Jehovah and 'publishing' his teachings are referred to as 'publishers'.

As previously mentioned, and according to JW.org, active publishers who preach 'the Truth' are officially counted as fully fledged members of the church. Publishers may be baptised or unbaptised. An unbaptised publisher may decide to get baptised (if they have not yet been baptised previously or in adolescence) as long as they are already considered to be an active publisher, that they share in as much preaching work as possible, and they have decided to dedicate themselves to Jehovah in prayer and want to serve Him forever.

Although baptism signals a Witness's ultimate commitment to Jehovah, once baptised they are forever exposed to the act of disfellowshipping, the ultimate punishment for a baptised Witness (discussed later in this chapter).

FUNDING

The church exists purely on anonymous, voluntary donations from individuals who are either Jehovah's Witnesses or generous, external benefactors. Contribution boxes are available at their various meeting places, and other ways to donate are explained on their online donations page. 'Separate options are provided so that a person can choose to donate for our worldwide work, for local expenses, or for both,' explains JW.org.

Jehovah's Witnesses are not expected to tithe or donate any specific amount of their income. They also do not take church-service collections or charge admission to their church gatherings. However, when donations are made, either by members of the congregation or by other benefactors, they are announced at church meetings with great fanfare and adulation, arguably appealing to the 'guilty consciences' of those who have not yet donated. All are welcome at church gatherings.

Watchtower's Brooklyn properties, which served as the organisation's headquarters since 1909, have proven far more lucrative than expected. These were sold off one by one after the headquarters moved to Warwick in upstate New York, releasing substantial amounts of cash for the organisation. As Evans writes in *The Reluctant Apostate*: 'Put simply, far from being a drop in the ocean, the income from the Brooklyn sell-offs was considerable and resulted from the milking of an enormous cash cow that has been steadily inflating over many decades.'

In addition to selling the Brooklyn properties, the construction of their new headquarters was made possible by voluntary funds, volunteer labour and various tax exemptions. As a registered non-profit organisation, Watchtower has enjoyed many tax benefits and subsequent cash savings. An online news report titled 'The Scientology Money Project' by Jeffrey Augustine, from 15 November 2018, claims that the Watch Tower Bible and Tract Society listed the book value of its assets as $1 451 217 000 on their 2015 IRS tax form. 'This places the Jehovah's Witnesses into the same "billion-dollar plus" cult status as the Church of Scientology.'

Interestingly, in their 2013 IRS tax form, the Watch Tower Bible and Tract Society listed their book-value assets as $675 419 000. This substantial increase of $776 095 300 in Watchtower wealth between 2013 and 2015 is accounted for by the sale of some of their most lucrative New York real estate. Even more interesting, in a separate line item on both forms, the Society lists its primary, unrelated business activity as 'Investment Activities'. 'So,' writes Augustine, 'while the rank-and-file Witnesses are striving to please Jehovah, the big boys at the top have sold over $700 million in prime real estate and ploughed that cash into undisclosed investment activities.'

BAPTISM

Jehovah's Witnesses who are born into the faith are not typically baptised at birth; rather, they are first taught the ways of Jehovah before actively committing to and partaking in their baptism. Once baptised, a Witness cannot reverse their decision without serious consequences, as baptism is the most hallowed of acts and the pinnacle of a Witness's dedication to Jehovah. Although children may be baptised from as young as eight years of age, this sacrament is typically reserved for those twelve years and older.

In *The Day of Jehovah's Witnesses*, Rebecca Walsh writes that children twelve years of age and even younger are accepted annually for baptism with the sole purpose of dedicating their lives to serving Jehovah. They are required to take irrevocable vows that could, potentially, place them in a vulnerable position because, as baptised members of their congregation, they are no longer considered 'children', but are expected to behave as adult Witnesses, susceptible to the same punitive measures that hang over the heads of their adult cohorts.

So, once baptised, children are considered wholly accountable for their actions and are thus vulnerable to the punishments of shunning or disfellowshipping should they stray from Jehovah's path and be found guilty of a serious transgression. 'Why would such young children put themselves forward for such a serious commitment?' Walsh asks. 'One reason could well be the relentless pressure placed on them from within the Organization of Jehovah's Witnesses.'

Should the prospect of disfellowshipping be too much to bear for a baptised Witness who has lost their faith, they may attempt to hide this transgression by simply dwindling into inactivity; they might try to live a life of obscurity without ever publicly denouncing their faith or admitting their disobedience to anyone in the hope that they can exist without attracting the attention of the elders and the Watchtower community.

However, no matter how secretively a disillusioned Witness may choose to live, it is always made clear that if one avoids confessing to the elders, one is doomed forever. One cannot lead a fulfilled or successful life until one confesses to the elders and before Jehovah. Either choice leaves the doubtful Witness in anguish.

DISFELLOWSHIPPING

Disfellowshipping is the practice of excommunicating a member from the Jehovah's Witnesses congregation for going against the doctrines and teachings of Jehovah and the rules laid out by the Governing Body.

Disfellowshipping comprises one of three outcomes: Private Reproval, where only the elders know the reason for the reproval; Public Reproval, where an individual is publicly reproved with an announcement at Kingdom Hall and the individual is removed as a serving member of the congregation, but is allowed to associate with friends and family; Full Disfellowshipping, where one is completely disfellowshipped and expelled from the congregation and may not associate with family or friends at all.

Disfellowshipping is typically reserved for baptised Witnesses (as the ultimate punishment for disobedience after baptism), and the individual is physically and emotionally shunned by every member of their congregation and their family. In extreme cases, the individual may not greet, speak or socialise with anyone in their congregation, including their own family members.

Usually, full disfellowshipping is a lifelong punishment, unless the individual is truly repentant and wishes to return to the fold. In that case, they may be allowed to return, but only after they have endured a considerable amount of shunning and humiliation and are able to convincingly demonstrate their repentance. On the JW.org website, disfellowshipping is explained as follows: 'Two factors – which must coincide – result in the disfellowshipping of one of Jehovah's Witnesses. First, a baptized Witness commits a serious sin. Second, he does not repent of his sin.'

In the foreword to Lloyd Evans's book, *How to Escape from Jehovah's Witnesses*, Paul Grundy, author of JWfacts.com, reveals that 'it is estimated that well over two million Jehovah's Witnesses have left the Watchtower organization since 1995', and that 'Jehovah's Witnesses have the highest turnover of any religion in the United States, with two thirds of those raised as Witnesses eventually leaving.'

Leaving the Jehovah's Witnesses Church is not an easy decision to make, because being disfellowshipped, shunned and forever separated from one's family is incomprehensible to most. Disfellowship renders an individual completely isolated and fearful, not to mention doubtful of their ability to survive outside of the church; in other words, disfellowshipping is a powerful deterrent. 'In my experience,' writes Grundy, 'ceasing to be one of Jehovah's Witnesses has led to post-traumatic stress disorder, depression and, sadly, even suicide.'

For the faithful Witnesses, the act of disfellowship has three core benefits: the disfellowship of wrong-doers honours Jehovah's name; it protects a clean, Christian congregation; and, most importantly, it potentially brings the transgressor back to their senses. Efforts might be made to re-accept the repentant ones, according to JW.org.

It appears then that the threat of disfellowship is a powerful weapon in Watchtower's arsenal of discipline, second only to the threat of Armageddon, in keeping their flock unconditionally committed, in line and under control.

A January 2022 online post by Hemant Mehta states that Norway took a decision in 2021 to stop all funding of Jehovah's Witnesses because of the 'religious sect's cult-like practices'. The Norwegian government found the practice of disfellowshipping especially troubling and deemed it to be both unlawful and unethical, particularly in how it may affect teenagers and young adults who are ostracised from their families at too young an age should they not adhere to the organisation's rigid doctrines. In response, the Jehovah's Witnesses organisation (JW.org) claimed that the actions taken against their church were not based on any 'expert opinion or court decision'. They claim that the government of Norway objects to their scriptural beliefs and practices regarding disfellowshipping, the governor going so far as to require them to change their disfellowshipping arrangement in order to keep their registration in Norway, but they maintain that such requirements have no formal legal or expert basis.

MARRIAGE AND SEXUAL RELATIONS

Marriage is considered the union between one man and one woman only, 'with sexual immorality being the *only* basis for divorce', according to JW.org. Abuse, in any form, appears not to be a good enough reason to seek a divorce. Furthermore, Watchtower literature condemns masturbation as a 'spiritually unhealthy habit', writes Evans in *The Reluctant Apostate*, and is considered self-abuse. Foreplay, anal sex, gay sex, and same-sex relationships or marriages are strictly forbidden.

Witness parents forbid their teenage children to partake in any sexual activity, including masturbation, before marriage. Teenagers are advised to make use of chaperones to ensure that they don't succumb to any 'unclean behaviour', writes Walsh in *The Day of Jehovah's Witnesses*. Walsh also claims that the Jehovah's Witnesses' uncompromising application of biblical teachings, which emphasise the sinfulness of sex before marriage, might push frustrated youths into early marriages as the only acceptable means of enjoying a romantic relationship.

It follows that couples who marry too young, and for the wrong reasons, run the risk of unhappy marriages and early divorce, the result not of 'wicked' external influences, but rather of the pressures exerted from within the organisation. Walsh poses this question: 'Is it moral for a society to pressure their teenage children into premature marriage, teenage pregnancy, and childbirth?'

WOMEN'S RIGHTS

Women do not hold positions of any material rank or responsibility within the Jehovah's Witness organisation. They are 'good' only for childbirth, child-rearing, homemaking and door-to-door preaching. 'The position of women within the Organization is one of submissiveness,' writes Rachel Walsh in *The Day of Jehovah's Witnesses*.

They are excluded from any congregational duties that involve stock-taking, financial accounting and record-keeping, but may perform cleaning duties in church and go onto the church stage to re-enact a 'door-to-door' preaching exercise. Women may not assume the position of an elder, regardless of how many hours, days and years they have spent walking the streets and knocking on doors. To this day, no woman has ever served on the church's Governing Body.

In *'Knock Knock' Who's There?*, Anthony James writes: 'Women Witnesses (referred to as "sisters") are considered "weaker vessels", and males (brothers) are viewed as their heads. Sisters are not allowed to take the lead in any congregational matters, including teaching, unless a baptised brother is not available.'

BLOOD TRANSFUSIONS

Jehovah's Witnesses are encouraged to seek the best possible medical care according to their needs. They are also not opposed to vaccination, which they consider a 'personal decision' for each Christian. 'We seek quality medical care and appreciate the many advancements of medical science to reduce the risk of serious illness,' states JW.org.

But then there is the contentious issue around blood transfusions, which the church regards as a religious rather than a medical matter. They draw their conclusion from the teachings in the Bible: that, as 'true' Christians, they should not ingest blood of any kind in any way. 'Both the Old and New Testaments clearly command us to abstain from blood,' claims JW.org.

For Jehovah's Witnesses, blood is sacred, thus the transfusion of blood from a donor, or from one's own stored blood, is strictly prohibited. In addition, blood may also carry certain diseases, such as hepatitis or HIV, which are an unimaginable prospect for a Witness. If a Witness accepts a blood transfusion or is even coerced into doing so by a medical practitioner, they run the risk of being disfellowshipped, especially if they do not express regret for their actions. Willingly and unrepentantly taking blood is not tolerated. If an individual is repentant, elders may decide to provide spiritual support and, after much penance, the individual may be forgiven.

A 2009 legal case in Johannesburg enabled a twelve-year-old Jehovah's Witness to receive a live-saving blood transfusion for leukaemia despite her and her parents' refusal to allow the procedure. With the legal opinion that the right to life presided over the right to religion, the young girl's doctors made an urgent application, and a Johannesburg High Court granted the order for the doctors to proceed.

The girl's parents ultimately respected the court's decision and her condition reportedly improved. This is one of many similar instances where doctors in South Africa have had to apply for a court order to override parents' refusal to grant life-saving blood transfusions in the best interests of a minor child.

In a more recent case, in 2019, parents of a ten-year-old girl from KwaZulu-Natal, who had sickle-cell anaemia and had to be admitted to a public hospital, also refused a blood transfusion and fought a court order for doctors to proceed. Doctors from a private hospital, respecting the wishes of the parents, then offered an alternative treatment protocol, to which the young girl responded well.

Although this case strengthens Witness parents' argument that they have the right to protect their religious beliefs, the broader medical fraternity, particularly in the public sector, argues that under emergency situations, parents should prioritise the best interests of their child over their religious beliefs, as alternative treatments may not always have the same positive outcome and, as medical professionals, they cannot and do not want to be responsible for avoidable fatalities. In the case of sickle-cell anaemia, public-health doctors argue that it is an unpredictable condition, and a blood transfusion would likely offer a better prognosis in the longer term.

One of the dilemmas facing a religious sect taking a vehement stand on a particular issue, particularly one related to medical care, is that it is difficult to reverse their position without some degree of embarrassment and, more importantly, without acknowledging responsibility for all the lives affected or lost while such a rule was in place. This is the problem the Governing Body of Jehovah's Witnesses currently faces regarding its stance on blood transfusions and the many Witnesses, including Witness children, who have unnecessarily given their life to preserve this decree.

Writes Evans in *The Reluctant Apostate*: 'The only thing they [Watchtower] can do is try to phase it out, so that gradually, without anyone noticing, blood becomes increasingly acceptable.'

Not surprisingly, with recent medical advances demonstrating that blood is not only made up of separate components, including white cells, red cells, plasma and platelets, but that these components may be singled out and utilised separately as derivatives of blood, Watchtower has begun changing its purist view on the nature and use of blood. Although blood transfusions are still prohibited, when it comes to the benefits of some of the by-products of blood, such as plasma, Watchtower states that each Witness should consider all the facts and make their own decision before Jehovah.

Watchtower commends the global medical community on their continued efforts to develop new methods of treating individuals who cannot have blood transfusions, including new ways of performing bloodless surgery. JW.org goes so far as to claim that 'many of the techniques developed for use in Jehovah's Witnesses patients will become standard practice in years to come'.

HIGHER EDUCATION

While Jehovah's Witnesses support a well-rounded education at both primary- and secondary-school level, they are less convinced of the merits of tertiary or university education. They believe that many university and college environments pose spiritual and moral dangers to their children and thus choose not to expose themselves or their children to such an environment: 'The university environment practices of what God condemns, such as drunkenness, drug use, and sex outside marriage, are often common and even encouraged,' laments JW.org.

Furthermore, 'mistaken ideas' and misconceptions are also believed to be promoted in these environments and, according to Jehovah's Witnesses, are misleading and in blatant opposition to the values of the Bible. JW.org's list of these ideas or misconceptions include: money brings happiness and security (money and materialism are constructs of Satan); a person should seek the prestige or status that can result from higher education (such a haughty attitude is exactly what Jehovah hates); each person should set his or her own standards of right and wrong (Jehovah's Witnesses only accept Jehovah's standards of right and wrong); and, finally, higher education is the best way to improve the world (God's Kingdom is the only hope for a better world).

JW.org goes on to say that: 'We recognize that many pursue higher education, not to gain wealth, prestige, or illicit pleasure, but to improve themselves and the world. These are noble goals, but Jehovah's Witnesses have chosen a different path. Like Jesus, we look to God's Kingdom as the only hope for a better world.'

Essentially, Jehovah's Witnesses believe that spiritual education, and even vocational training, ultimately hold greater value than secular education. Despite the small percentage of Witnesses, mostly young males, who go on to receive a post-school or university education, and even qualify as professionals, most still believe that their spiritual education has far greater value. In the words of JW.org, 'Unlike secular education, Bible-based spiritual education provides the life-saving knowledge of God.'

Perhaps, then, it is fortuitous that many other religions and non-Witness individuals do support higher education unconditionally. And, in so doing, populate the world with the many engineers, scientists, teachers, nurses, doctors and other invaluable professions that make it possible for us all to live and thrive – in particular, the building of engineering constructs like hospitals and Kingdom Halls, or the building and operating of aeroplanes and cargo ships that make global missionary work possible, or those who provide the life-saving medical care that Jehovah's Witnesses are so ready to accept.

SCIENCE AND CREATIONISM

Jehovah's Witnesses believe in creationism rather than evolution and its theories of natural selection and mutation. Jehovah God is the creator of all things, and all living things were created and have evolved through Divine intervention.

While they respect the achievements of science, Jehovah's Witnesses do not believe that science can answer all of humankind's questions. They firmly believe that all answers reside within the Bible and that a good education thus involves learning from both science and the Bible. JW.org states: 'At times, science may seem to contradict the Bible. However, some apparent contradictions are based on a misunderstanding of what the Bible actually teaches.'

DISASTER RELIEF

Jehovah's Witnesses are primarily focused on executing Jehovah's will and following his 'Truth' on earth. This includes getting involved in community work and disaster relief. Disaster relief, in particular, appears to have two main benefits for the Witness community: the first, and most obvious, is providing immediate physical relief to any of their members (and non-members) caught in a natural/physical disaster; the second, and less tangible, is providing emotional support.

Victims of a disaster are likely to be at their most emotionally and spiritually vulnerable and thus, arguably, more susceptible to emotional and spiritual influences. It is a good time to preach and convert. As JW.org explains: 'We provide practical relief assistance to both Witnesses and non-Witnesses, in harmony with the Bible's instruction at Galatians 6:10: "Let us work what is good toward all, but especially toward those related to us in the faith." We also try to give the emotional and spiritual support that victims sorely need at such times.'

While this seems both commendable and selfless, one might question the motives for such immediate and altruistic groundwork after disaster strikes, especially since the church's relief workers do so voluntarily, without pay, and without the support or backup of a sanctioned government body or aid agency.

Rushing to the aid of one's fellow Witnesses in times of crisis is understandable, especially given that their worldwide congregation totals just 8 million among 8 billion non-Witnesses; however, seeking to provide 'the emotional and spiritual support that victims sorely need at such times' may just be a stealthy ploy to maximise an opportunity to influence and/or convert the most vulnerable non-Witnesses. Consider the following online social post on *Quora*:

> Years ago, when my mother was dying, a JW came to my door. I explained I couldn't talk very long because I needed to get back to her, but I asked him to pray for us. He immediately bowed his head, so I took his hand in mine and listened as he prayed for us. He was sincere, generous, and beautiful and his kindness was a tremendous comfort…
>
> The Jehovah's Witnesses around here seem pretty organized and they are really nice. One lady came by about the same time each year and since she was trying to do what she thought was a good thing for me I always tried to be polite. She really had the sales pitch honed to perfection! She always had a way of using my objections or refusals as a way to keep the conversation going. Finally, I just was blunt. This isn't going to work, you need to stop wasting your time on me, I appreciate your good intentions, but don't come any more. She hasn't been back since. But oh my, she could sell ice to Eskimos.

OTHER LANDS

In *The Reluctant Apostate*, Lloyd Evans writes that Watchtower publishes an annual yearbook that contains a country-by-country breakdown of figures related to its evangelism work: 'A notable feature of the "Service Year Report of Jehovah's Witnesses Worldwide" can be found toward the end of the long list of countries and numbers. Positioned discreetly above the "Grand Total" is a row of figures attributed to "Other Lands".'

These 'other lands' refer to countries where Witnesses are banned or forbidden to preach or where they are punished if they endeavour to preach publicly. Although these countries are not named in the yearbook, Evans claims that it is relatively easy to identify them through a process of elimination.

As of 2015, these included Afghanistan, Algeria, Bahrain, Brunei, China, Djibouti, Egypt, Eritrea, Iran, Iraq, Jordan, Kuwait, Laos, Libya, Mauritania,

Morocco, North Korea, Oman, Qatar, Saudi Arabia, Singapore, Somalia, Syria, Tajikistan, Tunisia, Turkmenistan, United Arab Emirates, Uzbekistan, Vietnam and Yemen.

In a more recent Radio Free Europe report, dated 7 February 2019, four additional countries should be included on the list: The Comoros, Lebanon, Maldives and Russia. On the JW.org official site, their most recent report, the *2022 Country and Territory Report*, confirms this complete list of 'other lands'.

This is not to say that Jehovah's Witnesses do not attempt to do missionary work in some of these countries, despite the persecution or punishment they face. For some Witnesses, being imprisoned would form part of their absolute faith in and unconditional serving of Jehovah. There are currently only three countries where no Witnesses practise at all, namely North Korea, Somalia and Afghanistan.

According to the 2019 Radio Free Europe report, countries where Jehovah's Witnesses are the most active include the United States of America, Mexico, Brazil, Nigeria, Italy, Democratic Republic of Congo, Japan, Philippines, Zambia and Colombia.

CONCLUDING COMMENTS

Perhaps no one works harder than a Jehovah's Witness to spread their faith. Understated, committed and wholesome – foot soldiers for Jesus – unconditionally devoted, unquestionably disciplined and well-versed in socio-political neutrality. Most of all, they are obedient and faithful to Jehovah God and his salvation.

While other religions also deploy their members to complete missionary work to spread their 'truth', few partake in such a lifelong, all-consuming pledge of relentless serving, most notably the tireless drudgery of door-to-door and face-to-face Christian preaching. Walsh claims that 'Jehovah's Witnesses pride themselves on their strict adherence to moral principles and guidelines.'

Evans, however, points out that while other religions are commonly associated with scandal – the Catholic Church and alleged child sex abuse; Evangelical churches and their reported homophobia, misogyny and anti-science sentiments; and Scientology, a force not to be reckoned with after claims that they had turned their followers against their families and covered up millions of dollars in dubious tax-free donations – the Jehovah's Witnesses are not devoid of their fair share of disrepute either.

Over the years, allegations of paedophilia and sexual abuse against members of the Jehovah's Witnesses Church in their various global chapters have surfaced on different public platforms, but it appears that most of these have either been denied or gone under-reported by respective elders. Arguably, the now infamous two-witness rule may have potentially provided a convenient scapegoat to obscure claims of abuse, thereby perpetuating the so-called tactic of dismissing victims' cries for help.

Although not mentioned on the official website of the Jehovah's Witnesses, the practice of the two-witness rule is also not refuted. The 2016 Royal Commission into Institutional Responses in Child Sex Abuse enquiry stated that the Jehovah's Witnesses organisation 'relies on outdated policies and practices to respond to allegations of child sexual abuse' and that 'those policies and practices are not subject to ongoing and continuous review'.

The official enquiry went on to conclude that 'the organisation's retention and continued application of policies such as the two-witness rule in cases of child sexual abuse shows a serious lack of understanding of the nature of child sexual abuse' and that such policies and practices are, by and large, wholly inappropriate and unsuitable for application in cases of child sexual abuse. Whether this 'rule' is no longer practised in the church remains in dispute, but, as we will see later, in Maria's case, it was a contention when she reported her experience of sexual abuse to her elders.

Jehovah's Witnesses seem incapable of recognising or admitting that their policy of secrecy and the 'oppressive scriptural mores they place on their members' are enabling the problem, and that instead of protecting their 'flock', 'they are laying it wide open to abuse by unscrupulous predators within their ranks', writes Walsh in *The Day of Jehovah's Witnesses*. In Walsh's secular study of the Jehovah's Witnesses Church, she claims that 'if cases of child abuse are brought to their attention, the internal judicial system ensures that in many cases these offenses are not even reported to the relevant authorities. No professional help is sought when dealing with paedophiles, and scant attention is paid to the victims of their crimes.

Paedophiles are forgiven and reinstated at the whim of a body of men (the elders) with no relevant qualifications to deal with this kind of offense.'

Notably, a distinction should be made regarding allegations directed against the church as an institution versus members of it, particularly in terms of accusing it of systemic child abuse versus holding individuals within the organisation liable. In such instances the Jehovah's Witnesses Church has resorted to, and in some cases won, legal actions based on such allegations. For example, in a 2023 court judgment in the UK, the Jehovah's Witnesses Church won an appeal in the Supreme Court after a High Court judge had awarded damages to a plaintiff who was raped by a fellow Jehovah's Witness after evangelising door-to-door near Cardiff more than thirty years ago.

The *Independent* (UK) reported on 26 April 2023 that the plaintiff's attacker was an elder of the Barry congregation of Jehovah's Witnesses. She had sued for damages and claimed that the Jehovah's Witnesses organisation was 'responsible in law' for the rape.

After the Barry congregation of Jehovah's Witnesses appealed the verdict, Supreme Court justices ruled against the plaintiff and concluded that the 'Jehovah's Witness organisation' was not 'vicariously liable'. The High Court had been told that during an internal church inquiry in 1991 into the woman's allegations, a 'judicial committee' of Jehovah's Witnesses elders had found her allegations against her attacker to be unproven. Yet, more than twenty years later, the perpetrator was investigated by police and, following a trial in 2014, found guilty of rape and indecent assault and sentenced to fourteen years in prison.

Despite the plaintiff's claim that a 'proper' internal inquiry had not been carried out and that she believed leaders of the Jehovah's Witnesses were 'vicariously liable', the Supreme Court ruling stated that the rape had not been committed while her attacker was carrying out any duties as an elder on behalf of the church and that he had not been 'exercising control' over the plaintiff 'because of his position as an elder'. They further cited that 'there was no convincing justification for the Jehovah's Witnesses organisation to bear the cost or risk of the rape' that was committed by a single individual.

Jehovah's Witnesses believe that they pass the Bible's values that support their interpretation of morality on to their children, but while they claim to love their children, they may be failing to protect them from exploitation and abuse within their own ranks.

Jehovah's Witnesses' moral values are derived solely from Jehovah and his teachings – in their interpretation of the Bible – and they therefore shun any other source of information or educational instruction. Theirs, they believe, is the only religion in possession of God's 'Truth', which sets them apart from the rest of the world and protects them from the wickedness that befalls non-believers.

Maria's testimony of abuse, however, along with those of many other former Jehovah's Witnesses, potentially exposes another 'truth' that the Jehovah's Witnesses Church and some of its members are unwilling to acknowledge or do not want people to see.

CHAPTER 3

Rude Awakenings

Maria was six years old when she first encountered sexual abuse. Her father owned a holiday home in KwaZulu-Natal, and they invited friends of Donna's from her Jehovah's Witnesses congregation in Johannesburg to join them for the weekend. These friends comprised a married couple, of whom the father was a senior elder in the church, and their two young children. Maria describes this weekend as her 'first step into hell'.

On one of the evenings, the family's adolescent son suggested to Maria that the two of them play a 'fun' game of 'doctor-doctor'. He led the young and unsuspecting Maria into a bedroom, where he proceeded to touch her forcefully and inappropriately. Maria remembers thinking that it was not such a fun game; she felt uncomfortable and embarrassed. She left the room abruptly and went looking for her parents.

Too troubled to remain silent, Maria told them what had happened immediately, and, in the presence of the boy's parents, said that she did not enjoy playing with the young boy: 'I don't like the doctor-doctor game; it makes me feel sad and embarrassed.' Both sets of parents were shocked and, stunned into action, the boy's father grabbed his son aggressively, took him into another room and proceeded to beat him 'with a belt'.

Maria recalls hearing the young boy cry out in pain as his father unleashed his anger. The boy's parents then reasoned with Albert and Donna that although their son had behaved unacceptably, he was young and foolish and had been appropriately punished. 'So, as far as they were concerned, it was all sorted,' Maria says. With the incident now dealt with, the families continued with their weekend. 'It was all just ushered away.'

Although Albert was, in fact, quietly furious over what had happened, it was never spoken about again after that weekend. Donna's reaction was dismissive, which could have been ascribed to women's submissive role within the Jehovah's church, where they are not supposed to react openly to such incidents. Only the elders deal with transgressions of any nature. For Maria, it was an ominous foreboding of what was to come.

She mentions that that young boy reportedly grew up to be a sexual predator within the church, soliciting non-consensual sexual encounters with other young women, which eventually led to outright sexual abuse. Although he was eventually disfellowshipped by the church, he was not criminally charged. 'They did not view his behaviour as a crime, but more as a sin before Jehovah,' Maria explains. Within a few short years, however, having demonstrated sufficient remorse, the elders reportedly reinstated the young man into the church.

Maria believes he was allowed back into the congregation because his repentance had been so convincing; it was his ticket back into the fold: 'They never turn anyone away who wants to repent.'

From Maria's experience, to be revealed in more detail in the chapters that follow, and certainly from Jose Lopez's high-profile case against the church, it would appear that the Jehovah's Witnesses do not always practise what they preach. According to JW.org, the church 'abhors' child sex abuse, viewing it as a 'sin' punishable by Jehovah himself, rather, arguably, than a crime to be solely dealt with by authorities.

There appears further confusion regarding the actual reporting of sex crimes because while the Jehovah's Witnesses' official stand, as claimed on their website, is that they 'abhor child abuse and view it as a crime (Romans 12:9) and recognise that the authorities are responsible for addressing such crimes (Romans 13:1-4), and that elders do not shield any perpetrator of child abuse from the authorities', they also state that: 'In all cases, victims and their parents have the right to report an accusation of child abuse to the authorities. Therefore, victims, their parents, or anyone else who reports such an accusation to the elders are clearly informed by the elders that they have the right to report the matter to the authorities. Elders do not criticize anyone who chooses to make such a report (Galatians 6:5)' (JW.org).

It would appear, then, that child sex abuse is first and foremost regarded as a sin before Jehovah, and, as Jehovah God is the overarching authority in a Witness's life, elders do not necessarily obligate themselves to report allegations to external 'earthly' authorities (Jehovah will seemingly ensure punishment at the appropriate time) but rather the onus is on the individual to do so. However, if Maria's experience of excommunication from the church is anything to go by, one might approach the act of reporting abuses to external authorities with caution, with the possible threat of reproach or disfellowshipping.

Maria's high-school years passed with little further incidence. She recalls that during most of her school years, both in primary and secondary school, her one overshadowing memory is of shame and loneliness. She always felt like an outsider, embarrassed by her association with the Jehovah's Witnesses.

Her teenage years were consumed with Bible study and missionary work. From as early as the age of four, she had been groomed and trained for door-to-door missionary work. When she was very young, she would accompany Donna and Lara on certain days after school to carry out their preaching work. This entailed knocking on doors in their local neighbourhood to preach the word of Jehovah to anyone who would open the door and give them a few minutes of their time.

Each visit was recorded on a report card, detailing the time of the visit, the address of the house, who they might have spoken to, what questions they were able to field, if they left any educational material, and if there was any chance of a call-back or return visit, even if the person had refused to speak to them. On most of their visits, doors were closed in their faces. On one occasion, Maria, Donna and Lara were chased by a man carrying a shotgun who shouted at them to get off his property.

Door-to-door preaching is always conducted with a partner, either a family member or a friend from the congregation. The dress code is strictly smart and conservative: women in long skirts and conservative tops with modest hairstyles, the men clean-shaven and in suits. Beards are considered a sign of unkempt, rebellious behaviour.

The preaching work became increasingly traumatic for Maria after she turned twelve, not only because it was so time-consuming and was done without any regard for wind, rain or cold, but because of the bullying she suffered at the hands of her peers. At many of the homes, children from Maria's school would recognise her and, in the days that followed, she would be exposed to relentless teasing and bullying by the 'worldly' children at school, which forced an inconsolable Maria into complete social isolation. Then, in a few weeks' time, she, Donna and Lara would visit the same households all over again. The knock-knock/rejection/bullying cycle was relentless.

Interestingly, and relevant to Maria's rejection/bullying experiences, a 2014 *BBC News* article claimed that Jehovah's Witnesses have been adapting their preaching-and-converting modus operandi. In the UK, and across the larger cities of the US, particularly New York, Jehovah's Witnesses have reportedly been on a concerted drive to recruit commuters and passers-by as they go about their daily business. They now approach their potential converts on street corners, at busy train stations, at shopping centres and even in parks. This doesn't mean that they have abandoned their traditional door-to-door recruitment; instead, they see it as a 'progressive addition' to their usual recruitment tactics.

Handing out pamphlets, *The Watchtower* magazines and related paraphernalia at busy, highly populated locations enables passers-by to voluntarily interact with Jehovah's Witnesses rather than them having to actively pursue unsuspecting pedestrians. The Witness movement claims that this new approach has had a positive impact, as reported by Sophie Robehmed on *BBC News* in July 2014. Certainly, in this context in South Africa, one can observe, firsthand, how Witnesses go about 'God's work' at various strategic street corners and walkways in parts of Cape Town.

It was during this time, at around the age of twelve, that Maria was exposed to a second sexual encounter that echoed the same inappropriate behaviour she'd experienced at her parents' holiday house. An elder from Maria's congregation had offered to drive her home one afternoon after she had completed her missionary work for the day, when he suddenly pulled over, stopped the car, and asked Maria if she 'touched herself' and if she 'masturbated'. Maria didn't say a word, as she felt extremely awkward and didn't know how to answer the man. She didn't even know what the word 'masturbation' meant.

Not only was the question terribly embarrassing for the young girl, but it was also highly inappropriate for an elder to engage a young girl in this manner, particularly within the confines of his car. Maria is convinced that the man had ulterior motives – in the privacy of his car he was intent on achieving some form of sexual gratification. 'As young and naive as I was, it all just felt terribly wrong,' Maria says.

When she got home, she told her mother what had happened, but Donna took no further action other than to warn Maria not to tell her father. Donna said that it was better for Albert to be sheltered from such information, as he would otherwise either 'cause a scene' or question the authority of the elders. It was 'better' for him to remain protected from the church's censure, keeping in mind that the 'day of reckoning' would come, when Jehovah would unleash Armageddon. Maria saw this as nothing more than an attempt to hide the truth and prevent Albert from making a fuss at Kingdom Hall.

By the time she turned fourteen, Maria had moved to a private school in their neighbourhood and, desperate to fit in with her new schoolmates, refused to do any further preaching work. At the very least, 'I just refused to speak at the door. I kept quiet and let my mother and sister take the lead. I wanted to be as inconspicuous as possible.'

After two years, Maria moved schools again, this time to a much smaller private school, where one's background and religious preferences were of no consequence. Life became a little easier, and her last two years of high school improved marginally. Although Jehovah's Witnesses are discouraged from attending their matric dance, Maria managed to talk Albert into persuading Donna to let her attend.

'My parents had offered Lara the chance to host her own "matric dinner" with just her Jehovah's Witnesses friends. She had been very happy with this idea. My parents hired out a lovely restaurant and the whole affair was an exclusive "Witness"-approved event. As for me, I was having none of that. I wanted a normal school dance with my own friends. My mother wasn't happy, and the elders were even more disapproving, but it went ahead anyway. I put my foot down. It was the first time I had really stood up to my mother.'

Despite this small victory, Maria's ultimate goal was to finish school as quickly as possible: 'I just hated school. It didn't matter any more which school I was attending, I just wanted to get out of the whole rigid, competitive school environment. I needed to get out as fast as I could and avoid the Jehovah's Witness "label".'

At the start of her Grade-11 year, Maria decided to complete her last two years of school in one go. Combining her Grade 11 and Grade 12 studies, Maria completed the full two-year curriculum in a year. At the age of seventeen, with her school dance behind her, Maria matriculated and was finished with school.

CHAPTER 4

A Marriage from Hell

In Maria's household, the option to study further after school was not encouraged. Albert, however, insisted that she attend some form of tertiary college and study something that she would enjoy so that she could acquire a skill and earn a living. Maria had no such aspirations at that point, as her focus was exclusively on getting away from her home, her family and her church.

By this time, Albert's businesses in Johannesburg were expanding and he commuted regularly to the city for work. He was away from the family for long periods of time, and Maria felt alone and stifled in her mother's care. Donna was always pushing her into doing more Bible study and spiritual work: 'My mother and sister would gang up against me, forcing me to do more and more religious work, and they never missed an opportunity to tell me how I needed to put Jehovah first. If I put Jehovah first, nothing bad would happen – there was immense pressure. They were like a pack of hyenas whenever I came home.'

Like any young adult newly finished with school, Maria wanted to be more carefree and spend time with people her own age. However, they were not necessarily friends from the Jehovah's Witnesses congregation. With Donna's words ringing daily in her ears – 'You must put Jehovah first and everything will be rewarded to you' – Maria's claustrophobia exploded into outright rebellion. At seventeen, having just completed school and spent a few short months at art college, and still a minor in the eyes of the law, she left home.

It had never been an option for Maria to attend university. As the doctrines of Jehovah's Witnesses generally shun a university education, it was not a life path given any consideration in Donna's house. In a 2018 article by Samuel Osborne, published in *The Independent*, a former elder of the Jehovah's Witnesses congregation, who grew up in Poland, explained how women are regarded in their society:

> When asked how women were regarded in JW society, the former elder said they were thought of as 'a complement for a man', adding, 'She should be submissive to her husband, who is the head of their family, and it is he who makes all the important decisions.'
>
> Women cannot teach in the congregation; they cannot deliver public talks or say public prayers. When they conduct a private Bible study or say a prayer with another person, while a man is around, she has to wear a scarf on her head as a sign of being submissive.

In his book, *I, Witness*, Daniel Clark shares his experience of being dissuaded from pursuing a tertiary education, explaining that his family's Witness doctrine 'ran deep', with little thought given to his higher education. *The Watchtower* magazine had pointed out to his parents that although there may be student counsellors at school who would encourage the pursuit of a higher education or the consideration of various career opportunities in the 'worldly' system, it was both a pointless and dangerous pursuit and should not be attempted.

Instead of building a career, young Witnesses are expected to commit to missionary work. But, by placing spiritual needs above an education, young Witnesses run the risk of becoming unskilled and potentially unemployable, often with no alternative but to accept low-paying, often inconsistent work, rendering them financially exposed and conveniently more reliant on, if not entrapped, by the church.

For Donna, it was never a consideration that her daughters would attend university, but when Albert insisted that they obtain at least some post-matric qualification, he enrolled Maria at a local college that taught photography and graphic design. Unfortunately, it came to light that the college was not properly accredited to issue recognised qualifications and had no academic standing, and Maria snapped. She had finally lost all motivation and all residing faith in her parents – she packed her bags and ran away from home.

She explains: 'The church moulds you into their way of thinking. Nowadays it's not just no university, it is also no school. The Jehovah's Witnesses are advocating more and more for home-schooling to control the curriculum, increase and enforce scripture studies, and as a means of keeping their children insulated and completely dependent on the church.'

While Donna attended one of her usual church meetings, Maria grabbed a few personal items and met her boyfriend and his parents at an agreed rendezvous point. They would later come back to Maria's house to fetch furniture and more personal effects, but, for now, it was important to just go, to get as far away from home as possible.

Maria's boyfriend and his family were also Jehovah's Witnesses, but the father had been disfellowshipped. Her boyfriend's mother, on the other hand, was a strict, active member of the congregation. Maria fled to their home, which was only an hour away from Donna's, but it was distance enough. Maria was now an underaged 'runaway' without any source of income.

But desperate as she was to leave the clutches of her own Jehovah's Witnesses home, Maria had merely swapped one for another. She was now at the mercy of yet another Witness family, who at first tolerated her being there, as they were under the impression that their son and Maria intended to marry. But when Maria's 'new family' realised that she was not really interested in 'the Truth' or marriage, their hospitality quickly came to an end.

For a while, Maria worked as a part-time waitress at a nearby hotel and tried to establish some form of normalcy, but relations with her boyfriend's family, and with her boyfriend, soon soured. Within three months, around August 2005, they began arguing. One evening, the arguing escalated to such a point that her boyfriend 'became quite physical and kicked me out of his house in the middle of the night'.

Sitting outside the local McDonald's fast-food chain, Maria confesses that 'this was a really low point in my life. It was 2 a.m. and I was stranded and alone.' In the early hours of the morning, an acquaintance of Maria's made an uncanny, coincidental stop at the McDonald's drive-through and, recognising her sitting there alone and afraid, rescued her from the sidewalk.

The following morning, she drove Maria home, back to the visible disapproval of her mother. Although Donna was relieved to see her daughter home safe, she couldn't welcome her without a smug 'I told you so': 'She was almost glowing [because] I had returned home with my tail between my legs.'

The deal was that Maria could come home, but only on condition that she return to 'the Truth'. Donna showed no interest in why Maria had left home in the first place, only that she had come home and would return to the church. 'Looking back, I believe my parents always tried to look out for me and my mother's home was open to me, but she was never interested in why I had wanted to leave or why I was so unhappy.'

During her time away from home, Albert had bought her a new car, which he had delivered to her boyfriend's home. It was a fantastic surprise, but it came, yet again, with conditions ... and without car keys. If Maria wanted to drive the car, she would need to return home. But not even a car was enough to entice her.

'I had left a comfortable lifestyle in my parents' home, and now a new car, for a much lesser life, but none of it was enough to get me to return. My boyfriend earned little money and life was not fabulous or comfortable at all, but I wasn't willing to return. I was willing to leave my old life behind just to get away from the pressure of the church.' Only after she could no longer stay with her boyfriend's family and her situation had become somewhat destitute did Maria decide that she had no choice but to return home.

Very soon after that, towards the end of 2005, Maria's parents felt that it would be good for her to spend some time in Johannesburg to help in her father's businesses. It was a fresh start and a new career path. Her father was travelling between Johannesburg and Cape Town so regularly that he had established a comfortable home in which Maria could reside and re-establish herself. All of this, though, was dependent on Donna's demand that she join the nearest Witness community and return to the church.

'You always try to do your best for your children,' Albert says. 'Maria was a very artistic and talented teenager, but she was also headstrong and independent. She didn't like to be told what to do and was conflicted between wanting and needing her family and not wanting to lose her family, but then needing to pull away. She seemed to always have the pressure of her mother on one hand, and then me, her father, giving her advice on the other hand. She was always conflicted – it was tough for her.'

It was not long after Maria's arrival in Johannesburg in early 2006 that a local elder and family friend of her mother's began regular house calls to offer her both educational instruction and prayer sessions. This elder was none other than the father of the young boy who had inappropriately touched Maria at her parents' holiday house when she was six years old.

One of the conditions that Donna had laid down when Maria moved to Johannesburg was that she attend regular Bible-study sessions. 'My mother had hand-picked this particular "family friend" to enforce this, but his presence unnerved me and made me uncomfortable. I felt vulnerable all over again.' However, she was willing to make a fresh start in the church and, hopeful of pleasing her mother, she made a concerted effort to comply.

Maria knew the elder's daughter from family get-togethers and social gatherings over the years, and they were good friends. Maria welcomed this 'friendship', as it was a way to ingratiate herself with the local Witness youth community. She was hoping to experience a 'younger side to the Jehovah church' and find some 'lightness' in her new home.

Unfortunately, her hopes to establish a new social circle were quickly dashed. Put simply, Maria was not baptised in the Witness faith and was thus not yet worthy. The elder who had taken Maria 'under his wing' explained to her that she had to be baptised to be truly accepted: 'He told me that unless I was baptised, I would always be classified as Satan's child.'

He also instructed her to end any associations with 'worldly' friends and to keep her interactions with her father to a minimum. This was a brutal blow for Maria and a new low point. She had left her home in Cape Town to start a new life in Johannesburg, only to discover that she was not welcome in the eyes of the church unless she made the bold and irreversible move to be baptised.

'They lured me in, welcomed me at church meetings and personal study sessions, they made me feel welcome and affirmed that a new life and a new chapter awaited me. A new start was so close, it was "just around the corner" if I just did a little more, and a little more ... only to realise that I was branded "Satan's child", unworthy and unaccepted. Unless I got baptised, I was not welcome. They kept moving the milestones. I had tried so hard to fit in – this was devastating to me.'

Although Maria had done her daily Bible studies, memorised her daily scriptures, attended weekly ministry sessions to prepare for door-to-door missionary work, attended weekly Bible-study sessions as well as all Sunday services, she was still considered an outsider. She was, in fact, being shunned.

Maria felt manipulated, exposed and utterly alone – left to the wolves once more.

Why, then, did she stay? Why put herself through the self-recrimination, humiliation and doubt? Because, ultimately, change is difficult. In addition, there was the fear of being completely shunned and losing her family and friends, and the only community she knew. Kingdom Hall represented security and a sense of place and community. Maria knew that a different world existed beyond the gates of Kingdom Hall, she just didn't know how to access it or if she would survive in it. For Maria, it was a case of 'better the devil you know than the one you don't'.

The feeling of being a pariah in the eyes of the Witness community consumed Maria, and eventually she decided to stop trying so hard. At the time, she was living with her father, who was not involved with the Jehovah's Witnesses at all, and this made it easier for her to once again step away from the church. She stopped attending Bible-study classes, church services and youth meetings, and discontinued her personal scripture studies.

When Donna and Lara came to the realisation that Maria was turning her back on the church, 'they just cut me off and stopped all communication with me'. So, although shunned by her community, Maria was not disfellowshipped. 'I was often invited to attend church gatherings or partake in ministry work, or I would receive *The Watchtower* articles sent by congregation members, not as an extension of friendship or to be welcoming, but rather to ensure that I didn't stray too far from "the Truth". No one within my local congregation would take the time to befriend me, only the time to invite me back into the ministerial fold.'

It was during this time, living in her father's home, that Maria learnt of Albert's affair. Although she understood and respected his reasons for wanting a new and happier relationship with a woman other than her mother, Maria believed that Donna had a right to know about it, and that her father should communicate his new relationship to the rest of the family.

Albert, though, felt differently and was not willing to reveal his infidelity to his wife, not even at the behest of his youngest daughter. Maria remembers that he was adamant that she should not tell Donna: 'He threatened me with no roof over my head if I told my mother. I kept quiet, but it was difficult being torn between honesty to my mother and loyalty to my father. He was still my dad and my safety net.'

Although Maria was happy for Albert, keeping the secret from her mother upset her. It resulted in immense pressure and divided her loyalties between her parents. 'I felt like I was being ripped apart between my dad, who understood me, and my loyalty to my mom for being my mom.'

Slowly, cracks began to form in her relationship with Albert, and tensions mounted. The growing discord between father and daughter was significant, for soon Maria would need his protection more than ever. It was also significant for the role it played in her father's perceptions of why his marriage eventually broke down in the years that followed.

According to Albert, his wife's zealous, unconditional commitment to the Jehovah's Witnesses' doctrine had created an irreparable rift in their marriage, which affected their social and sex life, as well as their aspirations as a married couple.

One experience stands out for him: 'When we were first dating, I had an impressive collection of Chinese antiques and statues. One statue was [called] the "Goddess of Love" and of Eastern, Buddhist origin. Before our marriage, my antique collections never bothered [Donna], she had an appreciation for them, but after the Jehovah's Witnesses' philosophy began to take over her life, she complained that my collection of statues was offensive, that they had negative "energies". Their existence began to affect our marriage.' (Jehovah's Witnesses do not tolerate the worship or collecting of religious symbols or idols.)

'Because it had taken me a long time to put my collection together, I refused to get rid of it. Instead, to appease my wife, I put the entire collection into storage. But, after six months, there was no improvement in our personal or sexual relations.'

Maria had always made a conscious decision not to get baptised and, as a teenager, had refused to receive the sacrament of baptism on many occasions. Ironically, this had been her saving grace, as not being baptised meant that she could commit many 'offences', even withdraw completely from the church, but would always be welcomed back should she decide to return (however, not without due penance and repentance, of course).

Had she been baptised at the time she was living in Johannesburg and had then withdrawn from the church, she would have been disfellowshipped immediately, and being reinstated would have entailed a long and difficult process. At this juncture in her life, at the age of nineteen, Maria considered herself 'a goat among the sheep, just like my father'.

Then Maria met her first husband. We will call him John. 'Although raised in the Catholic faith, he was not a practising Catholic. It was only just before we got married, over two years into our relationship, that I became aware that he was a practising sangoma (witchdoctor), with a penchant for "black magic".'

John's lifestyle was the antithesis of Maria's – he represented everything that was free and uninhibited. With her mind in turmoil and desperate to break free of her suffocating surrounds and the disillusionment with her so-called friends and family, Maria was more vulnerable than ever. Raging to rebel and embrace all that was not pure, not safe, not controlled, Maria fell in love with this enigmatic man.

After dating for three years, Maria and John got married. Maria was twenty-two, and in the beginning, she and John had a happy relationship. They enjoyed each other's company, and John, who earned a comfortable income in the hospitality industry, spoilt her with gifts. He indulged Maria's love of all things artistic, encouraging her to draw and paint. Her creative talents had remained a steady hobby, but always in the background – not yet a cathartic outlet for her emotions. That would come later.

Maria's relationship with John resulted in many forgotten traditions from her childhood coming back into her life, like celebrating Christmases and birthdays, and enjoying various events over public holidays. After her move to Johannesburg, Maria had worked for her dad for a couple of years, but because his affair did not make for an easy or pleasant work environment, she moved on to work for other companies, acquiring proficient skills in the retail and corporate clothing industry, as well as in corporate events management.

As a result, Maria became more confident and self-sufficient. Things were looking up for her, and for the first time in a very long while, life seemed more colourful. Soon after her wedding to John, however, things began to change, albeit slowly and subtly at first. John's passion for traditional African medicine and his commitment to practising as a sangoma or 'traditional African healer' began to overshadow their relationship. (As practitioners of traditional African medicine, the name sangoma, originally a Zulu term, can generally be used to denote all types of southern African traditional healers.)

Maria became aware of John's 'hobby' just before they were married, but it didn't seem like a big deal at the time. In fact, as a sangoma, John had abandoned his Catholic faith, thus ensuring that for both Maria and her new husband, organised religion was no longer a feature in their lives. But the euphoria was short-lived.

To understand the significance of John's status as a sangoma, and what this would mean for Maria, a brief explanation of the practices of a sangoma is necessary at this point. A sangoma is a highly revered traditional healer among the Zulu and other tribal cultures of southern Africa. A sangoma's function is to diagnose and heal the physical, mental or spiritual ailments of individuals by performing various time-honoured rituals and ceremonies and prescribing herbal medicines.

Various forces, which can include one's ancestors, witches and sorcerers, are believed to have the ability to cause harm to individuals by way of evil spirits, or demonised living beings taking on the form of animals. Often, individuals will turn to their sangoma to perform rituals in which their ancestors are approached to appease the evil spirits. Sangomas are typically called to their vocation by a spirit, a calling known as *Ukutwasa*, which empowers the chosen individual with ancestral and cultural responsibilities that are used to protect and heal.

Although there are no gender constraints, most sangomas are female. While a sangoma's purpose is pure and 'divine', protecting those that fear bewitchment, and healing individuals from physical and mental ailments that cannot be cured by Western medicines, their abilities to communicate with loved ones who have passed embody a mystical power that can generate a dangerous, God-like omnipotence that can stray from the purest of intentions.

Medicinal potions and spiritual sacraments, intended to heal and protect, even break 'bad spells', can drift from the path of rightful intent to a darker side of magic and result in demonic rituals, dirty spells and satanic ceremonies that are used to control, manipulate and terrorise others, all in the pursuit of power and personal gain. For some, this dark magic and the 'spells' that are cast are very real and very dangerous. John was not just a practising sangoma – he dabbled in what Maria can only describe as 'black magic'.

A few months into their marriage, John's behaviour became increasingly strange and aggressive. He would often return home from work with a small cardboard box that Maria was never allowed to open. John explained that the box contained herbal medicines, traditional beads, a traditional healing cloth (in red, white and black), dried skulls of small animals and a very special necklace.

Maria says, 'I will never forget that necklace. Although the animal skulls were creepy, the necklace was symbolic of something more sinister. It displayed a small animal horn that contained "medicine". It was probably poison. [John] wore it all the time. He said it protected him from evil spirits, but it also instilled massive fear among his co-workers. It made me very wary and uncomfortable.'

In their first year of marriage, John would go away on 'sangoma rituals' for days at a time: 'At first, I thought it was all part of the spiritual practice, and being newly released from the overbearing, conservative confines of the Witness faith, I didn't sense any initial alarm bells.' Soon, though, and just a few months into their marriage, John started to display more worrying behaviour. He was practising 'darker' rituals, learning about casting spells and discussing the aura of 'black magic'.

Maria became scared and refrained from engaging with John on anything to do with his practice. This angered him and made him increasingly volatile towards her. He threatened to cast 'dark spells' on her and to make her life a 'living hell' if she didn't support and respect his way of life. He became suspicious, even stalking her when she ventured off without him.

Maria soon realised that it was an untenable situation and that it was unsafe to stay in their home, even to stay married to him. She had been warned that if she dared leave him, he would cast a 'deadly spell' on her, 'threatening to kill me if I left'. For a year, Maria planned her escape. In that time, John became so swept up in his 'calling', and so overwrought with a need to control and manipulate everyone around him, that he became physically abusive towards Maria.

'He would always insist on making dinner, but some evenings he insisted we eat in front of the TV in our bedroom. The next thing I knew it was early morning, and I would wake up with a pounding headache, my body bruised and sore all over, with evidence of his abuse all over my body. I suspected my husband was drugging me and then violating me.'

It was during this time, in early 2010, that the twenty-three-year-old Maria discovered that she was pregnant. On Mother's Day, 9 May 2010, 'I woke up to find John staring at me, a cold, dark stare. He told me, "You don't deserve to be a mother."' Maria was shocked and furious, and in the heated argument that followed, John shoved her down a flight of stairs. It would prove a fatal blow to her unborn baby. Maria was five and a half months pregnant.

Losing consciousness from the fall, Maria eventually came round to find John hovering over her and blaming her for losing his temper. Then he walked away. It was only three days later, on 12 May 2010, a date Maria will never forget, that John accompanied her to see a doctor. The doctor informed Maria that her baby girl no longer had a heartbeat, and that he would need to remove the unborn baby. 'John showed no remorse' and, unable to tell her family, there was no comfort from them either – she couldn't possibly tell her mother and sister what had happened. Maria suffered this tragic loss alone and in silence.

Devastated and terrified, she now knew she had to leave John: 'I was desperate to get out, but I had to be careful, because he'd threatened that he would come after me and my family, especially my dad. He said he could cast a spell from hundreds of miles away.'

Leaving her husband would not be easy, and the timing was critical. When the appropriate time eventually presented itself in 2012, almost two years later, Maria was ready. During a weekend when John was particularly aggressive, Maria had to barricade herself in her bedroom for safety. She phoned her mother in a complete panic, telling her that she thought John was going to kill her.

'My mom immediately phoned my father, who attempted to calm the situation down.' The following Monday, Maria made her escape: 'I told [John] that my car was not working and that I needed to borrow his to get to work to prepare for a function. With just the clothes on my back,

I disappeared in a matter of hours, without a trace. My father had organised a removal truck to collect my things that same morning while John was at work.'

By this time, Maria's relationship with Albert was too fractured for her to seek refuge in his home. She still believed that he should tell Donna of his affair and release her from the burden of keeping this secret from her mother and sister. Although Albert had sent removal trucks to get Maria's belongings out of John's house, she felt that she could not go back to his home. Also, she was afraid that she might lead John straight to her father once he realised that she was gone. So, Maria fled back to Cape Town and her mother's house.

'This was a very tough time for Maria,' Albert says. 'She had been through a very bad first marriage. I had advised her not to marry this man – he had a bad track record. It was frustrating for me to see her struggle so much and make the choice to go back to the Witness church. You try to advise your children, but there is only so much you can do.

'The Witness church presents itself as a refuge, but it takes over. They start slowly by offering friendship and solace, but then they take over your life. They always appeared to me, at first, to be "normal, ordinary" people – professionals, like lawyers and doctors, by day, but as you become involved with them, they start to take over your life, telling you what you should and shouldn't do. You start to lose your friends, your social circle and everything that you know. It's like being a member of an elite golf club – you are either a "true and committed player", a "true Witness", or you are not.'

Donna opened the doors of her home to Maria once more, but, of course, with the condition that she repent, come back to 'the Truth' and prove herself worthy once more. 'I had to beg my mother at first. She didn't want me to come back. After pleading to return and promising to come back to "the Truth", she welcomed me home.'

Maria didn't care any more; she was 'utterly broken'. She was in 'fight or flight' mode and just needed a place of safety, under any condition. 'I went back to my mother's house and begged her to let me come home. I barely remember what she said to me; I was just in need of refuge. I had hit rock bottom. I had lost my baby, and I was running for my life.'

Maria was almost twenty-five and destitute. 'Mom said that this had happened to me because I had left Jehovah and that I needed to experience all of this in order to see the light, to change my ways and to go back to "the Truth".' In hindsight, Maria believes that had her family given her the necessary support and acceptance, and not judged her, she might have walked away from her relationship with John sooner, and with greater confidence and a clearer head.

Despite being in an ill-fated marriage, Maria had managed to complete a beauty-therapist qualification, which now provided her with a means of earning her own income. Despite lacking in confidence and motivation, and depleted of energy, Maria tried to put her skills to work as a part-time therapist at a local health spa – and, surprisingly, loved it. In fact, for the first time in many months, she found that she had a renewed sense of purpose and direction.

In the background, though, there was still the matter of John: 'We had to convince John to accept a divorce and to stop threatening and stalking me. He still had my three cats and would threaten me that if I didn't return immediately, he would kill them one by one. It was unnerving and devastating to have him threaten my cats.'

Eventually, part-time work became full-time and, before long, Maria was thriving in her new position. Unfortunately, though, the demands of the Jehovah's Witnesses imposed once more. To keep her mother placated, and to try, yet again, to fit in, Maria resumed her weekly Kingdom Hall meetings and Bible-study sessions, falling naively, blindly, back into the 'faithful fold' that always promised safety, redemption and community: 'I was back in church in full swing to find a sense of place, some unconscious hope of drawing closer to Jehovah. My scripture readings ringing loud in my head: "Lean on Jehovah and He alone will sustain you. Throw your burdens onto Jehovah and He will protect you." The problem was that Jehovah didn't like it that I worked on Sundays.'

When Donna learnt that Maria had to work on Sundays, the elders were informed, and they vehemently disapproved (as did Donna). Maria had to request special permission from her employer to arrive late on Sundays, which compromised her job security. 'I wasn't forced into anything, but the pressure from my mother and the elders was palpable, and the consequences of disobeying were harsh (fear of recrimination and labelling). You just do what you know they want you to – I needed to go to church first on Sundays before starting work – it was just that simple.'

The pressure continued to mount as Maria's job became increasingly demanding with her growing clientele. Any days off work were spent either in Bible study, attending church or preaching 'the Truth' door-to-door. 'I would finish work at 6 p.m. and then still have to knock on doors preaching the word of Jehovah or have to attend two-hour-long meetings at Kingdom Hall. My newfound happiness was slowly being suffocated and eroded by the Witnesses again.'

Instead of the balance that Maria yearned to achieve in her new career, in her 'new life', she was being increasingly smothered by Witness rules and their judgemental reactions and unreasonable demands. 'I was being told what to do, and when to do it, where I could work and when, what social life I could have, even what books to read. I was told not to watch commercial movies – Harry Potter and *Lord of the Rings* were surely "demonic". Life was spiralling out of control again, again, again.'

By now, Lara was happily married and ensconced in the Witness church, her husband a ministerial servant and soon-to-be elder in their local Kingdom Hall. Enforced family 'nights in' were now added to Maria's exhausting schedule. 'Tuesday, Wednesday and Thursday nights were dedicated to Bible study, missionary work and family dinners – it was a relentless cycle that continued seven days a week.'

Maria remembers thinking: 'Where am I? I was numb, barely functioning, and completely depressed. The months just rolled on in this dark, unhappy space. I had a horrible feeling between being happy that my mom and sister were happy, but that I was so miserable.'

Maria had yet to properly process the loss of her baby and the devastation of her marriage, but, with Albert's help and financial assistance, she finalised her divorce. Maria had always felt that she could not fully disclose these traumatic events to anyone, least of all her mother, for fear of recrimination and further reproach. But still, she desperately needed release from all the pressure and trauma of her recent past.

Despite Donna's disapproval and the ramifications from the Witness community if she consulted a psychiatric specialist or a psychologist, Maria knew she had to do something – she was on a knife-edge. In 2016, she turned to a psychiatrist for help.

It was during this time that two major events coincided with Maria's mental breakdown: Albert filed for divorce from Donna, and Lara fell pregnant. For Maria, this was a bittersweet event, as her sister's pregnancy brought distressing, repressed memories of her lost baby girl to the fore. So distraught was Maria that she confessed everything to her mother – both the loss of her baby and the abuses she'd endured at the hands of her ex-husband.

Predictably, Donna's reaction was not one of sympathy; instead, she blamed Maria's 'misfortunes' on her shunning of 'the Truth'. 'Most days, I cried alone in my room. I couldn't eat, and I had terrible insomnia.'

In an ironic attempt to prevent Maria from turning her back on the church once more, and to subsequently safeguard her and her daughters' standing in the church, Donna made a reluctant conciliatory move to support her daughter's need for psychiatric help (Jehovah's Witnesses do not condone consultations with psychiatrists or psychologists). 'She wanted to keep me calm so that I didn't go off the rails completely and then leave the church again.'

Maria was prescribed a strong dose of sleeping tablets, as well as antipsychotics and antidepressants, all in the hope of addressing her depressive, suicidal thoughts and what she describes as her 'paranoia' – paranoia about being 'watched' and about her ex-husband finding or following her. But the medication just left her more exhausted and barely able to function. 'Some days I was so full of anger and rebellion, and on others so completely deflated and suicidal that I contemplated ending my life many times. I felt so alone, so worthless, so unworthy.'

In these dark months, barely holding things together, Maria found solace in her drawing, designing different tattoos that she had imprinted all over her body. They were a testament to her journey and a source of expression. They were also a source of immense emotional pain relief. The tattoos, however, were yet another 'taboo' for the Jehovah's Witnesses, who consider them a desecration of the sacredness of one's body. For Maria, these images were her catharsis, a rebellion of the highest order against a community that had summoned her and shunned her – today, these markings represent her story, her struggle and her triumph.

CHAPTER 5

Perdition

> 'Abuse has thus been called "the ultimate betrayal". We are reminded of Jesus' question: "Who is the man among you whom his son asks for bread – he will not hand him a stone, will he?" (Matthew 7:9) But the abuser gives a child, not love and affection, but the cruellest "stone" of all – sexual assault.'
>
> – JW.org

Despite going through an extremely challenging time, Maria had to earn an income and she somehow managed to start her own business as a beauty therapist, building a steady base of new clientele over time: 'I was emotionally numb during the day, but at night I would return home to my mother's house, lock myself in my room and collapse in a heap of tears. It was such a sad and difficult time for me, I don't know how I got through it all. But I had to work, and I needed to build my business, so I just went through the motions – that time in my life is quite a blur.'

By 2017, despite the success of her now well-established beauty-therapy business, Maria was barely holding things together. She masked her condition with a precarious reliance on anti-anxiety and sleep medications, but soon grew wary of all the pills she was taking and the emotional bluntness they caused: 'I had had enough of all the drugs and wanted to take back my life.'

By the end of that year, Maria had weaned herself off most of her medication, except the sleeping pills, but she remained vulnerable and emotionally spent, having lost 28 kilograms in just a few months: 'Two thousand and seventeen was a tough year – I was barely hanging on.'

In early 2018, Maria 'resurfaced' as a functioning member of her local Kingdom Hall, but her involvement in the church was non-committal and erratic, something that did not go unnoticed by her mother and fellow Witnesses. In March 2018, however, this was all about to change, because that month marked the 'Memorial of Jesus's Death', a significant global celebration in the Jehovah's Witnesses calendar: 'Once each year, Jehovah's Witnesses commemorate the death of Jesus just as he commanded when he said: "Keep doing this in remembrance of me" (Luke 22:19; JW.org).'

It was at a Memorial preparation meeting that Maria was reintroduced to her future fiancé. He was a familiar face in the congregation and someone who appeared to Maria to be just as 'lukewarm' towards his faith as she was – finally, a kindred spirit!

Maria explains that this young man was familiar to her because her mother and his grandmother had already tried to matchmake the two of them a year or two previously. After church meetings, they had interacted socially, but at that time Maria had found him overly flirtatious, rough-handed and overbearing: 'I was not keen on his forwardness.' At the preparation meeting of the Memorial of Jesus, however, he seemed very different. Maria was pleasantly surprised and a little intrigued. We will call him Simon.

Like Maria, Simon was neither an elder nor baptised; he was a bit of an outsider, and he, too, was looking for love: 'Mom convinced me [that] he was a good match.' So, Maria, still feeling like she was on an emotional collision course, depleted of self-esteem, was unenthusiastically curious and agreed to one date. 'I hated church gatherings. I had to really talk myself into this, but when we met up and he hugged me, it was a warm embrace, something I hadn't felt in a long, long time.'

They met at the beach for a picnic in a public place in broad daylight. Nothing seemed untoward. The date was uneventful but went well enough. At one point, Maria thought, 'Maybe he is a good guy. He's easy to talk to, and he seems completely smitten with me – maybe I've been wrong about him all along.'

On reflection, though, Maria admits that something was off. She had a nagging feeling that he was trying too hard to impress her, and that he was possibly being a little fake. 'I should have listened to my instincts, but I wanted to please my mother, to listen to her for a change, and I liked the idea of having company, someone to spend time with outside of work and church.'

For their second date, just a few days later, Simon took Maria to his family home to spend time with his parents. Donna was also there, which was not unusual for a Jehovah's Witnesses courtship. The excitement in the air was unmistakable and bordering on feverish: 'I could sense a weird kind of eager tension. His parents and my mom were so chatty and pushy about Simon and me, asking all sorts of questions about our "relationship" and our future plans. I couldn't quite grasp why they were so enthusiastic, but it all became clear soon enough.'

After dinner, Simon's mother announced out of the blue that Simon and Maria were getting engaged and that a wedding would probably take place in the coming months! As Maria explains: 'It is proper to date only if there is a view to marriage.'

Maria was completely stunned. This was a jaw-dropping moment of disbelief. Although Simon seemed pleased and not in the least surprised, Maria was completely taken aback, unsure of what had just happened. Was this a joke? Throughout the evening's events, Simon's father was quiet and appeared somewhat withdrawn; he was not particularly close to his son at the time.

Maria recalls that she was 'shocked into silence, overwhelmed by well-wishes and congratulations. Simon looked incredibly happy, and his mother was elated. My mother, too, seemed thrilled. It was the most surreal, out-of-body experience. I was just so shocked.'

Shock, doubt, warning bells ... these were quickly pushed to the back of Maria's mind. Overwhelmed with the contagious excitement around her, she didn't have the resilience to question or contemplate what had just happened. Instead, she allowed herself to be swept along in the euphoria of the moment.

Marriage would mean an opportunity at a new life, with someone who appeared to be a good match. He seemed kind and loving, and he was financially independent. She would need to get to know him better, but, after all, he was a Jehovah's Witness – how bad could it be? Surely it would be a marriage based on mutual respect and loyalty, things she'd never experienced in her first marriage. Somehow, it seemed plausible at the time, but looking back, Maria admits she had been completely ambushed.

'I was so broken at that point in my life that I just went along with it. I didn't know who I was, coming out of a terrible time of paranoia and loneliness. Going off all my medication was the worst cold-turkey experience ever, and the worst sense of loss I had ever felt. I wasn't sure what I wanted any more. I had been living in a vacuum for so long and he [Simon] was offering a new path – maybe now, my family would back off.'

The next week, Maria and Simon went shopping for an engagement ring. They chose a diamond that Maria could now design into a ring of her choice. There was just one problem: the diamond had a massive inclusion (crack).

'Simon explained to me that he had chosen the diamond on purpose. For him, it was symbolic because he felt nothing is perfect, we are all imperfect beings, and thus the diamond had significance. It was such a weird, unromantic thing to say, and it didn't do much to dispel my doubts.'

A damaged diamond would prove the least of Maria's worries, and at the time she decided not to make a fuss; it wasn't the end of the world, or so she thought. But it did cast a sad spell on their engagement. 'More alarming was the fact that the ring symbolised our "imperfection" – it was a warning that, unfortunately, I didn't heed at the time.'

It is difficult to imagine why Maria, after such an abusive, dysfunctional first marriage, was hurtling towards a second one with such doubts plaguing her and a 'flawed' ring on her finger. But she explains: 'It was a path I felt I should take but also one that was being "forced" on me by my mother and [Simon's] family and I really didn't have the emotional strength to resist. What else did I have going for me? All I could hear in my mind were the words: Jehovah! Jehovah! Jehovah! Give everything to Jehovah and he will take care of you!'

Simon was not an elder, nor a typical Witness, and if she was going to marry anyone, especially a fellow Witness, it might as well be him: 'If I was going to marry someone in the faith it would need to be someone like him, as he was less conservative and less strict – that, at the very least, was hopeful.'

Another week, and another family dinner at Simon's house. Again, Donna was present, and Simon's family was as welcoming as ever; in fact, they seemed almost *too* eager: 'There was more than just wedding fever in the air – there was a real sense of urgency about setting the wedding date and getting the plans into place.'

Things were moving at a pace, and Maria felt rushed into making decisions about guest lists, catering and scripture readings. Why the rush? Why the pressure? Maria was exhausted at the family dinner, and watching her mother finish another glass of wine, she knew that it would be a long evening.

Donna had seemingly long since acquired an affinity for alcohol, and that evening, surrounded by friends, was not unlike any other 'spirited' social gathering of the past. Donna was a devout Jehovah's Witness who enjoyed her tipple, which was ironic but, according to Maria, not unusual: 'Despite Jehovah's Witnesses' disapproval of tobacco and alcohol use, many senior Witnesses in our congregation still indulged in "prohibited" vices.'

Maria excused herself and drove home to her apartment. 'As I arrived in my driveway, something was off – my cats weren't there to greet me, and the night air was very still.' As she climbed out of the car and approached her front door, Maria was suddenly aware of a movement in the shadows and someone running towards her: 'He was crouching and running very fast.'

Maria fumbled for her keys, opened the front door in a panic and slammed it closed behind her. Moving quickly to a side window, she saw three men brandishing torches and wearing head scarves in her driveway. She knew immediately that they were robbers who had been waiting for the right moment to attack. Maria pressed the panic button in the house and telephoned Simon.

When Simon arrived, he was carrying what seemed like a loaded gun, which Jehovah's Witnesses are forbidden to carry or own. Once he was sure that the apartment was safe and that Maria was no longer in danger, he suggested that she sleep over at his parents' house that night. Still shaken by the experience, she was thankful for the offer. She explained to Simon that she still took sleeping pills at night to help her sleep: 'And once I take my sleeping tablet, I go into a deep sleep – I am out for the count.'

The following day, Simon and his parents insisted that Maria move permanently into their home. They had a guest cottage on their property, which Simon occupied, but if Maria chose to move in there, he would move back into the main house.

Everyone agreed that this would be the safest option until the wedding day. 'His mom was very pushy. She wanted our marriage signed and sealed and seemed very keen for me to live on their property, under their influence, and to finalise the wedding plans.'

At this point, it is perhaps best to remember that Jehovah's Witnesses only condone divorce in the case of adultery, and not for any other reason. Within a week, Maria had moved out of her flat and into the cottage, safely ensconced within the family compound. Simon's father even drew up plans to modify their garage to accommodate a home salon for Maria.

Everything appeared to be coming together: Maria now had a loving fiancé, a welcoming family and a brand-new salon. Despite everything being so rushed, it was also quite exciting. Maria thought it better to let go of her anxieties and mistrust of the world. If she could stop resisting Jehovah and let him into her life, then maybe he would take care of her? 'I felt so special. Even though it was rushed, and his parents were being pushy, it felt so good to be cared for.' With Maria's future laid out effortlessly before her, it still seemed too good to be true: 'I had a nagging feeling that I should run.'

Within days of moving in, and just a few weeks before their nuptials, the pre-wedding socialising with family and Witness friends intensified. Maria, though, was still haunted by the traumatic memories of her recent past and her only solace was that she was a stickler for routine and got regular sleep (always with the help of strong sleeping tablets).

Despite the constant socialising, Maria maintained her routine: 'Since we were not yet married, we were not allowed to be alone, without chaperones. I found the constant company of others, almost every night, too draining, and so I would excuse myself by 8.30 p.m. and go to bed. I would always take a sleeping pill; they were a godsend at that time and the only way I was able to get a decent night's sleep.' Simon knew Maria's routine like clockwork. Unbeknown to her, he also had his own key to the cottage.

Late one evening, long after Maria had gone to bed, Simon let himself into the cottage. He'd apparently told his parents that he wanted to watch a sporting match on television and didn't want to disturb them. Since Maria would be asleep, he would just watch the game at the cottage and then return to his own room.

Even though Simon's family were respected senior members of their Witness congregation, it was so close to the wedding day that his mother apparently 'allowed it'. For Jehovah's Witnesses, however, rules are rules, and Simon should have been chaperoned.

Maria recounts: 'Simon came over to the cottage where I was asleep. He let himself in and closed the door behind him, and that is when it happened. When I woke up the next morning, I just knew something was not right.'

She awoke to find bruises on her thighs and down her legs: 'Almost like handprints. My body ached and my legs felt stiff. I had a sick feeling in my stomach and a weird recollection of what I thought must have been a dream. I felt sore and uncomfortable, like I might have a urinary infection.'

Maria and Simon had agreed to wait until after they were married before sleeping together. Maria wanted to do things right this time around, to do things the 'Witness way'. But it had been a mutual decision. 'For someone who was "saving herself" for her wedding night, I just knew something had happened while I was asleep, not just physically, but this feeling of weird flashbacks was all too familiar.'

Feelings of dread and denial flooded Maria's thoughts as she showered and dressed and tried to piece together the events of the previous night. She and Simon had a lunch date. She would have to confront him.

As soon as they were alone in the car, Maria turned to Simon and asked: 'Did something happen last night?' Simon, seeming very calm, shifted in his seat and said: 'Well, yes, kind of, don't you remember? You were gagging for it. But don't worry, no one will know. Just don't say anything. It's fine.'

Maria went still, dead still. Her mind was racing: this could not be happening ... Simon was her fiancé, and a Jehovah's Witness, no less ... how could he have done this? Memories of John flooded back into Maria's head, his indignation and anger that would so often lead to physical rage. She decided not to say anything right then. She felt nauseous, yet she had no clear memory of the night before. She stifled a tear and they drove on in silence. Lunch that day was a blur.

An article in the Jehovah's Witnesses' *Awake!* magazine in Watchtower's Online Library reveals that only the Bible holds the solution to ending sexual abuse: 'Jesus summed it up: Love God with your whole heart. Love your neighbour as yourself (Matthew 22:37-39). The apostle Paul repeated it: Love does not work evil to one's neighbour; therefore, love is the law's fulfilment (Romans 13:10).'

The article states that this solution of brotherly love is both logical and practical and, when applied, effective. Watchtower preaches that one needs to practise what one believes, not merely just believe it. The article ends with the following mantra: 'In God's due time all who embrace His kingdom under Christ will become able to keep this law of love perfectly. Then will come fulfilment of Proverbs 2:21, 22. This is the only way, the final way, to end the abuse.'

In the days that followed, Maria had to decide what she wanted to do, and she had to decide quickly. The wedding date was drawing closer, and the congregation was increasingly expectant. Reliving the events of her past, Maria went into survival mode. Not wanting to spark a row, she told Simon and his parents that she was feeling overwhelmed and needed space.

Since her old apartment was still unoccupied, she moved out quickly and was able to create some distance for herself: 'I stayed in my apartment, I locked the doors and I didn't answer my phone, despite numerous attempts by Simon to reach me. I could only think of his betrayal – nothing of what had happened was consensual. How could I possibly spend my future with this person?'

Maria told Donna and Lara what had happened. To Maria's surprise, Lara was disgusted and supportive of her decision to break off the engagement. Donna, however, remained quiet and contemplative. Because Lara's husband was an elder, he told Maria that she would have to inform the elders of what had happened. He told her that the elders would handle it.

Three elders from the local Kingdom Hall were assigned to hear Maria's case. They insisted that they visit her at her apartment and a date was set for the 'hearing'. Maria was not allowed to have any member of her family present on the day. Instead, she found herself alone in her apartment with three strange men, two of whom were middle-aged and the other in his mid-seventies.

Maria was asked to tell them when and how she was assaulted. She was grilled for what felt like hours about the event. Even though she was not fully conscious during the assault itself, she was nonetheless asked to provide as many intimate details as possible of what she *thought* might have happened. The elders even enquired what sexual positions Maria thought she and Simon had used, and which sexual acts Simon would likely have performed on her.

'They asked me questions like, was there foreplay involved? Why and how do you think you had sex? Was it vaginal or anal? Did he ejaculate inside you? Do you think you might have got pleasure from it?' They also asked Maria about the injuries and physical wounds she'd suffered. Again, she was asked to provide as much detail as possible: 'I was forced to provide every last detail, leave nothing out; [it was] hours of graphic interrogation.'

In her home, alone with three strange men, discussing the most intimate and private details of an unsolicited and non-consensual sexual act was humiliating and mortifying beyond description. It seemed nothing more than a sinister and manipulative tactic not only to debunk and derail Maria's accusations, but also to shame her at the same time.

'Claiming rape was tricky because I could not remember the events,' Maria says, 'but I thought they would be empathetic and would accompany me to the authorities. Instead, they wanted me to describe the most intimate details of my physical state the following morning; they wanted to know what my genital area felt like, what it looked like ... it was the most demeaning and humiliating experience of my life – worse than the assault itself.'

After the interrogation, Maria asked them why she had to answer these questions – what was their relevance? The elders replied: 'My dear, we have to ask these questions to make sure you are repentant.'

Maria was completely stunned. She felt like she was being assaulted all over again. Since she had been unconscious for most of the ordeal and could remember little of it, she started to doubt herself. Was she somehow complicit in her own rape? The elders were certainly implying that she had been responsible for Simon's 'transgression': by moving into his home before they were married, she had 'invited temptation'. It was an arrangement that Jehovah would not have condoned, they said, and Maria should never have agreed to it. This despite the fact that her future in-laws, senior members of the Witness congregation, had insisted that she do so, and had been so welcoming that it was easy for her to accept their offer. In other words, Maria was to blame because she had accepted their 'hospitality' and thereby 'enticed' immorality.

Just like that, the focus of the interrogation had shifted. The blame for what had happened was placed firmly at Maria's door. It was not Simon who was in the wrong, but rather Maria's weakness and lack of discipline that had created the opportunity to entice a young man who could not control himself. Maria was the Jezebel.

The elders asked Maria if there was a witness to the crime, someone who could corroborate her story: 'Because without a second witness, it would be difficult to confirm the incident.' Of course, there was no second witness.

The elders appeared to think that if there was no second witness to attest to the crime, it probably never happened ... or at least not in the way that Maria claimed it did. Either way, the way the elders saw it, it could not be confirmed that a crime had been committed. Also, unless Simon came forward to admit to committing rape, it would, in their minds, be almost impossible to determine the veracity of Maria's claim.

Without a second witness and a clear memory of the events, and without a formal confession from Simon, the elders informed Maria that there was no satisfactory reason for them to take action against him. They informed her that they would meet with Simon and hear his side of the story and, once they had all the facts, would come to a decision. No one mentioned reporting the 'incident' to the authorities. Instead, the matter would be handled within the church. Maria was then dismissed, and the three elders left her apartment.

In his book, *I, Witness: The Shocking Insider Story of Jehovah's Witnesses*, former Jehovah's Witness Daniel Clark reiterates the reported existence of the two-witness rule and further claims that, in the absence of a second witness, for a charge of sexual abuse to be taken seriously by the church, a confession by the alleged perpetrator is required. Although sexual predators don't typically commit their crimes in public places in front of other people, the idea that the perpetrator would willingly confess is equally absurd. However, the most alarming edict of all is that the victim must 'demonstrate resistance' to the attack. Clark writes: 'Before January of 1964, rape was considered "wilful fornication" and a reason for being disfellowshipped if the victim didn't scream.' However, in January of that year,

Clark writes, the Watch Tower Society decided that screaming was not necessary to validate a claim of rape. But then, in 1969, it was further declared that 'a woman could once again be dis-fellowshipped if she reported a rape, but admitted she didn't scream. This continued to go back and forth over the years.'

Today, the criteria of 'screaming' and 'resistance' to determine a case of rape are not addressed or defined on the Jehovah's Witnesses' official site. However, contention regarding the continued existence of the two-witness rule (confirmed previously in the findings of the 2016 Royal Commission Report and more recently in the UK's Independent Inquiry into Child Sexual Abuse (IICSA), released in 2022, and discussed in a later chapter), and that it is still a group of men who decide if the criteria for rape have been met, remain perturbing practices reminiscent of fifteenth-century witch-hunts.

During her ordeal, Maria could not turn to her father for comfort, and she was even less inclined to seek any from her mother. Instead, the incident with Simon was so raw and shocking that she again internalised her emotional trauma. To this day, Albert is unaware of all the details around the incident.

'I didn't know much about the incident at the time,' he says. 'And of course, there was no rape kit or evidence that she could use against this man. But as time goes on, I am learning more and I want to be there for her, although, as a father, you don't necessarily want to hear all the details; it is too difficult. I just want to be there for her – she has been through so much and I am so proud of her.'

Albert revealed another story that not only bears relevance and a striking resemblance to Maria's interrogation by the elders but is also a testament to his own fury and sadness over the church's behaviour. During his marriage to Donna, their eldest daughter, Lara, was summoned to a meeting with the elders over claims that she had been promiscuous with a young boy from the Witness congregation. Albert recalls having to take Lara to the local Kingdom Hall to attend a meeting with the elders, but that he had not been allowed to accompany her into the interrogation room.

So, Lara went in alone, and three or four elders interrogated her for what felt like hours. 'Because I was not allowed in,' Albert says, 'there was no way of protecting her. She left the room crying and we never really spoke about that time again. No doubt, she had been privately and severely reproved.'

In the matter of Maria's and her sister's similar experiences with the elders of the Jehovah's Witnesses Church, it is both interesting and relevant that the church claims to hold the following position on sexual abuse and child protection (JW.org):

- Elders strive to treat victims of child abuse with compassion, understanding, and kindness. (Colossians 3:12) As spiritual counsellors, the elders endeavour to listen carefully and empathetically to victims and to console them. (Proverbs 21:13; Isaiah 32:1, 2; 1 Thessalonians 5:14; James 1:19) Victims and their families may decide to consult a mental-health professional. This is a personal decision.
- Elders never require victims of child abuse to present their accusation in the presence of the alleged abuser. However, victims who are now adults may do so, if they wish. In addition, victims can be accompanied by a confidant of either gender for moral support when presenting their accusation to the elders. If a victim prefers, the accusation can be submitted in the form of a written statement.

By the time Lara wed a prospective elder in the Witness community, she was firmly reinstated in the church. Albert, as a non–Jehovah's Witness, was not allowed to walk his daughter down the aisle. Instead, he had to sit quietly at the back of the church and watch helplessly as she gave her heart to her husband and her soul to the church.

In the weeks that followed Maria's 'confession', she felt a void, a quiet emptiness of 'what now?' Fortunately, Simon had stopped calling by then and his parents had also withdrawn, yet this new 'quietness' had its own ominous undertone.

With no word from the elders, and absolutely no plans to get married, Maria officially broke off their engagement.

About three weeks after the elders' interrogation, Maria was summoned to a second meeting, at Kingdom Hall. This time, there were five of them. The elders told Maria that they had reached a conclusion. They then informed her that there was insufficient evidence to take further action. More importantly, Maria should be aware that she was not entirely without blame, as she had willingly moved into Simon's parents' home, where he also lived, and had 'obviously encouraged' his behaviour.

At the Thursday church meeting that followed, Maria was reproved in front of the entire congregation for what was deemed 'immoral behaviour'. Without revealing to the congregation the details of what had happened, Maria was 'named and shamed' for conducting herself in an immoral and sinful fashion in front of everyone she knew. Although not completely disfellowshipped, she was relegated to the back of the church and instructed to limit her interactions with the rest of the congregation until the elders saw fit to reinstate her as a full-serving member. Simon, on the other hand, received a private 'slap on the wrist'. His behaviour was documented and filed away, not to be discussed ever again.

In Watchtower's Online Library, the literature explains that 1 Corinthians 5:11 reads: 'Stop keeping company with anyone called a brother who is sexually immoral or a greedy person or an idolater or a reveller or a drunkard or an extortioner, not even eating with such a man.' According to JW.org, these individuals should not be received into one's home, nor should anyone socialise with them, for those who greet or socialise with them 'is a sharer in [their] wicked works'.

CHAPTER 6

Sexual Abuse: A Crime Against the Flock

'Children are a sacred trust, "an inheritance from Jehovah".
(Psalm 127:3.2)
Jehovah's Witnesses abhor child abuse and view it as a crime.
(Romans 12:9)
We recognize that the authorities are responsible for addressing such crimes (Romans 13:1-4).
The elders do not shield any perpetrator of abuse from the authorities.'

– JW.org

Sexual abuse, in all its guises, is an abhorrent crime and seemingly endemic in our modern society. It has no regard for age, gender, race, ethnicity or socio-economic status. Child sex abuse is arguably the most deplorable, and historical evidence of such crimes has become increasingly prolific across a variety of religious denominations, particularly among Christian-based faiths.

In February 2023, *Euronews* reported the following: 'Over the past seven decades, more than 4,800 children were sexually abused within the Catholic Church in Portugal, according to a report by an independent commission released in February 2023.' More alarmingly, the same report revealed that the Catholic Church would 'release a list of abusers that are still active'.

While historical allegations of child sex abuse, dating as far back as the 1950s, within the Catholic and other Christian-based faiths continue to come to light, there is little confidence that such abuse has been stemmed.

Within these Christian-based denominations, parents tend to encourage their children to participate in church activities for the positive spiritual experience of fellowship and worship, yet, in many cases, they unwittingly and potentially expose them to opportunistic sexual predators. Sexual abuse in any form is indefensible, but perhaps especially so in Christian-based ministerial services that encourage a variety of extracurricular youth activities, including Sunday schools, youth camps and choir services.

In *The Day of Jehovah's Witnesses*, Walsh claims that when the scandal of child abuse erupted in the 1990s in the Roman Catholic Church, Jehovah's Witnesses 'were quick to point an accusatory finger and count it as proof of corruption within the ranks of the Church'. Yet now that similar cases have been exposed within their own ranks, they deny any wrongdoing or corruption on their part.

Many cases of child abuse within the Jehovah's Witnesses community have come to light in recent years, garnering notoriety in the public press. A 2012 scandal involved Candace Conti, who was molested repeatedly when she was nine and ten years old by a member of the North Fremont congregation of Jehovah's Witnesses in California. A jury awarded Conti $28 million in damages in a landmark ruling, the biggest-ever amount awarded to a single victim in a religious child-abuse case.

Walsh writes: 'What is depressing about the situation highlighted by the Conti case, is that Jehovah's Witnesses seem incapable of recognizing that the policy of secrecy and the oppressive scriptural mores they place on their members are part of the problem, and that far from protecting their "flock," they are laying it wide open to abuse by unscrupulous predators within their ranks.'

Allegations of child sex abuse within the Jehovah's Witnesses Church have been stacking up steadily around the world since the early 2000s, and many of the cases reflect the same harrowing, humiliating experiences Maria endured: emotional bullying, sexual coercion and abuse, exploitation and emotional neglect.

In 2022, four Jehovah's Witnesses from four separate Pennsylvania congregations were charged with sexually abusing nineteen children in unrelated cases over a period of nearly twenty years. The charges included indecent assault, rape and involuntary deviate sexual intercourse, as reported in October 2022 by *Religion News Service*.

A spokesperson for the Jehovah's Witnesses reportedly said they agreed with calls for victims of abuse to consider contacting the police. 'As

Christians, Jehovah's Witnesses despise the mistreatment and abuse of anyone, especially precious children. While it is not appropriate to comment on cases pending before the courts, we want to express our concern for all victims of abuse regardless of faith.'

In one of the cases, the accused molested six young girls, including his own daughter. 'His daughter testified in court that her mother would remind her to lock her door at night if her father was around,' the publication reported.

In another of the cases, the accused allegedly used sexual molestation to discipline his daughter, who reportedly told other members of her congregation, including her mother, that she was being abused. No action was taken. Her father was charged with endangering the welfare of a child, aggravated indecent assault, rape and involuntary deviate sexual intercourse. After he was charged, he took his own life.

In the United Kingdom, in 2018, more than a hundred people contacted *The Guardian* with allegations of child sexual abuse and other mistreatment in Jehovah's Witnesses communities across the UK. The publication reported on claims by former and current members, including forty-one alleged victims of child sexual abuse, who described a culture of cover-ups and lies, with senior members of the organisation, 'known as elders', discouraging victims from coming forward for fear of bringing 'reproach on Jehovah' and being exiled from the congregation and their families.

In Europe and other parts of the world, recent international studies such as the Australian Royal Commission, the UK Charity Commission, the UK's Independent Inquiry into Child Sexual Abuse and the University of Utrecht in the Netherlands, have all reported on alleged child sexual abuse among Jehovah's Witnesses.

This grave situation is arguably enabled by the closed nature of the Witness community, as well as constitutional religious rights that exist in many Western countries that allow church organisations a degree of religious autonomy to conduct their own internal investigations and disciplinary proceedings, separate to and often above 'the law'. This is a privilege that may be exploited by religious organisations, including the Witness community.

As a result, incidents that take place within the organisation are often not made public. Furthermore, children who grow up in the sheltered community of the Jehovah's Witnesses where tertiary education, let alone sexual education, is largely shunned, are poorly equipped to deal with sexual abuse, particularly sexual acts at the hands of their elders who are deemed trusted, anointed vessels of Jehovah. In such a context, very young children may even confuse sexual abuse with love and duty. Young boys and girls also probably feel they cannot question or share their experiences with others to seek help because talking about sexuality is taboo.

The UK's Independent Inquiry into Child Sexual Abuse (IICSA), officially launched in 2014, released its final report in 2022, confirming that systemic abuse is apparent in all religious groups across the UK, citing 'blatant hypocrisy' and 'moral failings' in the way major UK religious groups handle child sex-abuse allegations. It examined evidence from thirty-eight groups, including those from Christianity, Orthodox Judaism, Islam, Sikhism, Hinduism, Buddhism and non-conformist Christian denominations. 'The report found that leaders discouraged reporting abuse to protect reputations.'

It also revealed that religious leaders tend to blame the victims for their abuse. The IICSA report found that many religious groups were putting children at risk by victim blaming, not openly discussing matters of sexuality, religious leaders abusing their power, men dominating the leadership and misusing the concept of 'forgiveness' to keep abusers within the fold.

The IICSA investigated more evidence regarding the Jehovah's Witnesses in England and Wales than any other group: 'The organisation has repeatedly been accused of covering up child abuse and told the inquiry allegations concerning 67 individuals had been reported to its branch office within 10 years.'

Of particular significance in the inquiry was the IICSA's criticism of Jehovah's Witnesses' biblical rule requiring that two witnesses confirm an incidence of abuse before the allegation can be considered by the elders. The Jehovah's Witnesses gave evidence that it also has policies requiring that allegations be reported to the police when there is a legal duty to do so. However, the UK has no such mandatory reporting law. In 2021, *BBC News* reported as follows: '[The] IICSA strongly criticised the "two-witness rule", saying it was likely to increase the suffering of victims, and failed to reflect the reality that "child sexual abuse is most often perpetrated in the absence of witnesses".'

In response to earlier findings in the IICSA report, Jehovah's Witnesses UK released the following statement:

> The protection of children is of utmost concern and importance to all Jehovah's Witnesses, and they fully agree that all religious organisations should have a child protection policy. We will carefully and respectfully consider all the observations and recommendations contained in IICSA's investigation report.

THE TWO-WITNESS RULE

> 'In case there should be found in your midst in one of your cities that Jehovah your God is giving you a man or a woman who should practice what is bad in the eyes of Jehovah your God so as to overstep His covenant ... you must also bring that man or that woman who has done this bad thing out to your gates, yes, the man or the woman, and you must stone such one with stones, and such one must die. At the mouth of two witnesses or of three witnesses the one dying should be put to death.'
> – Deuteronomy 17:2-6 (quoted in Walsh, *The Day of Jehovah's Witnesses*)

In the Jehovah's Witnesses Church, children, teenagers and, as we have witnessed in Maria's case, adult women have little recourse to justice when a crime is committed against them, as the perpetrators are often protected by the church's internal disciplinary system. There is no independent jury or judge, only an unjustifiable insistence on the two-witness rule. When does the sexual abuse of a child typically occur out in the open for anyone else to witness? In the Jehovah's Witnesses' system, the victim is exposed to being twice victimised. 'Once again, the morality of the Bible falls far below that of the contemporary world,' says Walsh in *The Day of Jehovah's Witnesses*.

A 2016 UK report in *The Guardian* describes the anguish of a victim who was too scared and embarrassed to report her abuse to the elders of her local community. She was four years old when she was abused and only told her mother many years later, when she was fourteen. Her mother then reported it to the elders: 'All the while I had it hanging over my head that if I wanted to raise any allegations, I would be forced into a judicial committee, I would have to confront [the abuser] face to face.'

Having to face one's abuser, especially without the support of a credible witness, is a humiliating and traumatising experience. Although the church can disfellowship anyone for minor offences, sexual abuse is apparently tolerated, and without a second witness to support the accuser's claims, the cases are dismissed. As *The Guardian* article reported: 'Had they discovered he was playing the lottery, he would have been disfellowshipped without question, but he admitted to them he had abused children, and he still wasn't disfellowshipped.'

A UK spokesperson for the Jehovah's Witnesses responded as follows to *The Guardian* article: 'Anyone who commits the sin of child abuse faces expulsion from the congregation... Any suggestion that Jehovah's Witnesses cover up child abuse is absolutely false.'

In the same article, in a related case, another woman, 'Jane', who also sued the church after she was raped as an adult in 1990 by a fellow church member, claimed that 'she was urged to face her rapist at a private hearing known as a judicial committee. It left her "completely traumatised" and led to the breakup of her marriage.' Her attacker was eventually jailed in 2014. Again, a spokesperson for the Jehovah's Witnesses claimed: 'We are in no position to, and neither would we wish to, force any victim of abuse to confront their attacker.'

Another report, in July 2017 in the *Manchester Evening News*, tells of three victims of a convicted paedophile in Manchester, England. As children, they were molested by a Jehovah's Witnesses elder and were made to attend a church committee meeting, where they were 'interrogated by the man who molested them and forced to relive their experiences in detail as eight other senior congregation members looked on'. The perpetrator already had a criminal record for abusing two little girls in 2013, for which he had served jail time. Despite his criminal history, he was reportedly considered 'repentant' following his release from prison and allowed, at that time, to return to the congregation.

'At the time of the interrogations, a whistle-blower told the *Manchester Evening News*: "Before each meeting the women were read a scripture on false witnesses and told to consider it carefully. They had to go through the abuse in detail and were asked if they encouraged it. One of the victims was asked if she had enjoyed it.'"

Across the seas, in the United States, yet another lawsuit reveals how elders at a Utah congregation of Jehovah's Witnesses allegedly forced a fifteen-year-old girl to listen to a recording of her rape as part of an internal church inquiry. The case, originally filed in 2016, stated that the leaders of a Witness congregation in Roy, Utah, made a teenage girl 'sit and listen to the recordings for hours in 2008 as part of a religious inquiry', as reported in November 2020 in an *Independent News* article.

The girl claimed that a fellow church member had raped her three times. The church launched an investigation into the accusation in early 2008, where the elders called the girl and her parents into a committee meeting to determine whether the girl had solicited the attack and 'engaged in sinful conduct'. Without the corroboration of a credible second witness, the victim was left completely exposed. 'During the committee meeting, the elders played the recording "on and off for hours" in an attempt to extract a confession.'

Despite the countless articles, reports and lawsuits, the Governing Body of the Jehovah's Witnesses stands firm in its belief that sexual abuse, including the abuse of their most vulnerable members, their Witness children, is not tolerated, and that perpetrators are accountable not only to Jehovah, but also to the full might of the law.

On their official website, JW.org, a detailed two-page document lays out their position on child sex abuse. Titled 'Jehovah's Witnesses Scripturally Based Position on Child Protection', this document defines child abuse as behaviour that may include neglect, physical abuse, sexual abuse or emotional abuse. Considering the few cases shared in this chapter, arguably a fraction of the many more that might exist, the following two statements in the Jehovah's Witnesses' document are particularly significant:

Statement One:

Elders strive to treat victims of child abuse with compassion, understanding, and kindness. (Colossians 3:12) As spiritual counsellors, the elders endeavour to listen carefully and empathetically to victims and

> to console them. (Proverbs 21:13; Isaiah 32:1, 2; 1 Thessalonians 5:14; James 1:19) Victims and their families may decide to consult a mental-health professional. This is a personal decision.
>
> **Statement Two:**
>
> Elders never require victims of child abuse to present their accusation in the presence of the alleged abuser. However, victims who are now adults may do so, if they wish. In addition, victims can be accompanied by a confidant of either gender for moral support when presenting their accusation to the elders. If a victim prefers, the accusation can be submitted in the form of a written statement.

From Maria's personal experience, neither of the two statements ring true: 'They do not encourage mental health practitioners because they do not believe in the same scriptural views as the Jehovah's Witnesses.' Maria was not allowed an accompanying confidant or family member when she made her case against Simon.

In James Anthony's book *'Knock, Knock' Who's There? 'The Truth' About Jehovah's Witnesses*, he describes another widely read Jehovah's Witnesses' book, *Shepherd the Flock of God*, which is a dedicated manual for elders, but which contains further concerning information regarding the handling of sexual abuse, particularly the sexual abuse of children.

The manual claims that 'the rules regarding what constitutes adequate evidence for judicial action include the following: "Even though a Christian is accused of wrongdoing serious enough to require judicial action, a judicial committee should not be formed unless the wrongdoing has been established. Confession. Admission of wrongdoing, either written or orally, may be accepted as conclusive proof without corroborating evidence. (Josh. 7:19) There must be two witnesses to a confession, and the confession must be clear and unambiguous."'

The manual further explains that a guilty plea entered in a court of law by a Christian (a Jehovah's Witness) as part of a plea bargain to secure a lesser penalty is not in itself regarded as an admission of guilt by the congregation. In addition, 'there must be two or three eye-witnesses, not just people repeating hearsay; no action can be taken if there is only one witness'. If there are two or three witnesses to the same kind of wrongdoing but each one is witness to a separate incident, the elders can consider their testimony. While such evidence is acceptable to establish guilt, it is preferable to have two witnesses to the same occurrence of wrongdoing.

Of particular concern, James explains, is how the 'two-witness' rule is applied to the most heinous of acts: paedophilia and domestic violence. The rule's only purpose is to protect the perpetrator. 'More importantly, the "Flock" book does specifically discuss child molestation and has the following to say: "Child abuse is a crime. Never suggest to anyone that they should not report an allegation of child abuse to the police or other authorities. If you are asked, make it clear that whether to report the matter to the authorities or not is a personal decision for each individual to make and that there are no congregation sanctions for either decision. Elders will not criticise anyone who reports such an allegation to the authorities."'

What is astounding in this text is how someone in a position of authority, such as an elder, does not have to absolutely *insist* that a victim go to the police.

James writes: 'It is deeply troubling that this is not the case within this important handbook. Upon examination, it seems likely the only reason this line is in place is to legally protect the Watchtower Society from blame, rather than to protect children. In addition to the above, there is also a clause that enables someone to "get away with" serious acts by waiting until a much later time to reveal them. "... if the immorality or other serious wrongdoing occurred more than a few years ago and the individual is genuinely repentant and recognizes that he should have come forward immediately when he sinned, good counsel by elders may be sufficient."' The last sentence is quoted from page 74 of *Shepherd the Flock of God*.

Shepherd the Flock of God appears to expose the many loopholes that senior members of the Jehovah's Witnesses might use to their own advantage in their pursuit of 'righteousness' and 'cleanliness'. For James, 'it is another example of a corrupt man-made system that enacts autocratic control of its subjects, while simultaneously teaching and enforcing contradictory rules and regulations as it sees fit'.

CHAPTER 7

Disfellowshipping

> 'There were three elders telling me I had encouraged my rape. I had never asked for permission to move in with Simon. Apparently, I had put myself in that situation and now I had to repent.' – Maria

Blamed and shamed, Maria was resigned to her fate. At this point, she not only gave in to the admonishments and recriminations meted out by the elders, but she also gave up emotionally: 'I accepted my punishment from the elders. I just thought: "Say and do whatever you want" – I was so sick of it all.' After the previous two years of depression, suicidal thoughts, loneliness and insomnia, she had run out of energy.

Reflecting on her marriage to John and now the end of her relationship with Simon, Maria couldn't help but think that this was the second time in her life that she found herself sexually assaulted by a 'trusted' partner – was there something in her psyche that was driving her to make bad choices? Maybe the elders had a point: Did she knowingly put herself in a vulnerable position and therefore had some part to play in her own abuse?

Lost in self-doubt, Maria had no fight left in her: 'I was just done. I took my punishment, removed myself as an active member of the congregation and sat at the back of the church like a naughty child.' Taking any further action against the elders would have risked being disfellowshipped, and Maria was not willing to accept that fate – at least, not yet. 'You cannot and must not fight back with the elders – you can get immediately disfellowshipped. For me, at this time, it would have been the worst option, so I kept quiet and went along with their decision.'

After her public reproval in May 2018, Maria withdrew from her church community but decided not to do anything that would further annoy the elders. She knew she had to keep a low profile and demonstrate genuine repentance. As a 'shunned' woman, she would need to be extremely mindful of her actions. For the next couple of months, Maria focused on her beauty-therapy business and kept her 'head down and didn't cause trouble'.

Although she had not been disfellowshipped or completely shunned, she remained publicly reproved and, as such, was expected to show remorse and repent her actions. Of course, her congregation had not been made fully aware of what those 'actions' entailed: 'When I was publicly reproved, the elders did not say what the reproval was for, only that I had "misbehaved" in the eyes of Jehovah and needed to correct my ways.'

This sent the rumour mill into a spin, and the congregation immediately began to gossip. 'Gossip is a huge issue in the church,' Maria says. 'Immediately after the public announcement of my reproval, tongues started wagging and phones started buzzing. There were loads of text messages filled with speculation and gossip. Every Witness congregation would know what had just happened. There was nowhere to hide from the shame.'

Maria's congregation knew of her engagement to Simon, but now that the engagement was off and she had been publicly reproved, they needed a story. The Witnesses started creating their own narrative of what had happened between Maria and Simon. The story was embellished so many times that eventually everyone 'knew' that she had 'obviously' had sex before marriage. As the vicious rumours were circulated among her Witness congregation, many of its members – friends included – stopped talking to or interacting with Maria. She became a pariah.

Idle gossip is an all-too-common social pastime, but it has the potential to cause immense damage to the person concerned. Jehovah's Witnesses are not immune to gossip, even though they condemn it outright as the Devil's work, according to JW.org. In fact, gossip is systemic in the global network of Kingdom Halls and is shared at nearly every church meeting and field-service gathering, and not just among local congregations but also the wider global Witness community. As an empty source of entertainment for the often bored, but so-called spiritually 'cleaner' members of the Jehovah's Witnesses, it is manna from heaven.

An article in Watchtower's Online Library, titled 'Gossip Can Destroy You', explains that 'gossip started with the Devil. Eve listened to his slanderous tale about Jehovah, believed it, acted upon it, spread it to her husband,

and the final result was that the first human pair was separated from their best Friend. From that time to this, men have gossiped, and men have suffered for it.'

Few, if any, have not been guilty of it or been victimised by it. Often, those repeatedly guilty of it are the most indignant when they become its target. 'Really, we should not be ignorant of Satan's devices. We should be on guard against gossip, a weapon of the Devil,' preaches JW.org.

Watchtower claims that gossip is aimed at causing injury; even harmless statements, when repeated, can become harmful as the embellishment of a story often leads to inaccuracies and falsification of the truth. JW.org: 'Jehovah's command: "You must not go around among your people for the sake of slandering"; "You must not take up an untrue report"; and "You must not follow after the crowd for evil ends." Even though an untrue report is repeated by many, we do not have to follow that crowd and join in slandering our brother. Thus, talking about others and their misgivings or their transgressions, is not acceptable behaviour and is not the way of Jehovah: "One who discloses secret matters of no concern to others is speaking foolishly, is meddling, busy bodying, talebearing, gossiping."'

However, there appears to be a double standard in the literature around gossiping on JW.org. According to the Jehovah's Witnesses, there are circumstances when a secret must be told, even though someone could get hurt or injured as a result. In this scenario, it is no longer considered gossip, but rather the necessary action of any responsible Witness: 'When you know someone is secretly sinning and jeopardizing his standing with Jehovah and marring the purity of the congregation, you must speak.

'In some cases, it may be sufficient to speak to the individual involved; more often it will be necessary to talk to the servant committee of the congregation. To make such a report may result in what seems injurious to the guilty person, but actually the ultimate result will be to his good.'

So, while it is wrong to gossip, it is sometimes apparently 'right' and expected that a Witness report on any 'sinful' behaviour he or she observes in a fellow brother or sister. Reporting on another's transgression – what most of us would consider to be disloyal gossipmongering or 'snitching' – is absolutely encouraged: 'Jehovah's law provided for witnesses to testify against wrongdoers. We are not forbidden to bear witness; we are only forbidden to bear false witness. Many in the world condemn as "squealing" the disclosure of facts that expose another.'

Furthermore, JW.org explains: 'In the Christian congregation it is a mistaken sense of loyalty to a brother to shield his sins when those sins jeopardize both his life and the congregation's purity. The true friend of the brother and of Jehovah's congregation will rebuke him, or, if necessary, will report to the committee so that a rebuke of greater force can be given to shock the sinner back to his senses. A true friend will inflict this temporary wound for the sinner's eternal healing.'

For Witnesses, the lines are clear: it is not considered gossip to report to the elders the sinful behaviour of another; it is only gossip when such news is spread to others in the congregation who are not in a position to take corrective action. Of greater significance, though, is the claim by Jehovah's Witnesses that it is the women in the community – and not the men – who are seemingly the guiltiest of gossip. JW.org again: 'Though it may not be pleasant for women to hear, the Bible seems to indicate that women trespass with the tongue more often than men. This is not to say men do not gossip. They do. Some gossip more than women. But women as a group are guilty of gossip more than are men as a group.'

The Jehovah's Witnesses website goes as far as to claim that the Bible specifically warns against women's characters, implying that they lack intellectual fortitude and are the 'weaker sex': 'At the same time they [women] also learn to be unoccupied, gadding about the houses, yes, not only unoccupied, but also gossipers and meddlers in other people's affairs, talking of the things they ought not. Not the male tongue, but the female tongue is the one singled out as the irritant in households. A wife's quarrelling is a continual dripping of rain. And a continual dripping on a rainy day and a contentious woman are alike; to restrain her is to restrain the wind or to grasp oil in his right hand."'

Watchtower goes on to say that although men don't necessarily have higher principles than women, women do tend to enjoy talking about 'mundane' things; women typically prefer to talk about people, which may lead to gossip: 'Men are more interested in subjects, in science, world events, economics or their work, and when they talk about these things the danger of gossip is not so great as when discussing people.'

So, while women are considered the real perpetrators of gossip, and gossip is apparently not tolerated in the church, a report in a 2018 *Independent News* article by Samuel Osborne reveals a different scenario. Here, the victim was a former elder of a Jehovah's Witnesses' congregation in Poland who had lost his faith and begun challenging his elder colleagues. As a result, he was denounced and disfellowshipped, after which such vicious, distressing rumours circulated about him among his former congregation that he allegedly took his own life: 'He felt so pressured that he jumped into a river and killed himself.'

The same article also reported that women in the Jehovah's Witnesses Church are thought of merely as 'a complement for a man', a vacuous but necessary companion, and, as such, should observe the 'laws of submissiveness'.

'She should be submissive to her husband, who is the head of their family, and it is he who makes all the important decisions. Women cannot teach in the congregation; they cannot deliver public talks or say public prayers. When they conduct a private Bible study or say a prayer with another person, while a man is around, she has to wear a scarf on her head as a sign of being submissive.'

Not only is gossip alive and well in the Witness community and, seemingly, a well-crafted mechanism covertly encouraged for the purposes of controlling and humiliating fellow Witnesses, it is women, no less, who, when so-called 'responsible reporting' morphs into gossip, are painted with the 'gossip brush' – the seemingly weaker, more 'tainted' members of the Witness congregation.

But while women are seemingly the perpetrators of gossip – 'the Devil's work' – there are men in the congregation who appear capable of far worse. If idle gossip is the work of the Devil, what, then, do Jehovah's Witnesses make of blatant sexual exploitation perpetrated by male Witnesses against the female members of their congregation?

In 2017, Maria accepted a client booking from a middle-aged man from her local Witness community. He was, in fact, a married elder who 'had booked for a back, neck and shoulder massage. That was all he could afford,' Maria recalls.

He arrived for his appointment carrying a small bag. Maria ushered him into one of the treatment rooms and asked him to disrobe and lie down on the massage table. The elder complied, but he had one 'small request'… He opened the bag he had been carrying and produced a set of skimpy lingerie. He asked Maria if she wouldn't mind wearing the lingerie while she did the massage.

'I calmly said NO, that I run a professional business and nothing like that was allowed in my salon. He looked embarrassed but said nothing. He then lay down and I proceeded to give him a massage. When the massage was over, I left the room. He got dressed, paid for his treatment and left without a word.'

Maria was not particularly surprised by the incident, but she was also not going to stand for such a solicitation: 'Honestly, I don't know what he was thinking. Maybe because I had been reproved and the rumourmongers had insinuated that I might somehow be amenable to such behaviour he thought he could request something like that…I don't know, but he certainly left my establishment embarrassed and in no doubt that his request would not be tolerated.'

Towards the end of 2018, a close friend of Maria's from a Witness community in Gauteng, who had himself become disillusioned with the church and had been disfellowshipped, left home and moved to the Western Cape, where he'd accepted a job as a local farm manager. Unfortunately, though, he was epileptic, and soon after his arrival at his new job, he suffered a near-fatal seizure. The owners of the farm managed to locate his mobile phone and dialled the most recent number on his call list, which was Maria's.

'They phoned me in a panic; they didn't know who else to call, [so] they just phoned the last dialled number on his phone. They told me [that] he was lying on the floor and appeared to be unconscious. He had likely knocked his head during the fit. His head was bleeding.' Maria explained that he was a former Jehovah's Witness and that she would have to call his parents.

Although his parents had distanced themselves from their son because he had been disfellowshipped, Maria knew that they were the only family he had, and she thought they would surely still be willing to help. Her friend needed emergency medical attention and had to get to a hospital as quickly as possible.

Maria called her friend's parents and told them that their son had had a serious seizure and appeared to have suffered some brain trauma, as he was unable to speak or sit up, and his head was bleeding. She asked if they could arrange for an ambulance to fetch him. She would then meet the ambulance at whichever hospital he was taken to and wait with their son until they arrived.

With no medical insurance, no family nearby and the owners of the farm in a total panic, Maria was sure that her friend's parents would spring into action: 'To my absolute shock and disgust, they told me that their son was disfellowshipped. He needed to learn a vital lesson. This was how Jehovah punishes anyone who leaves his flock.' They refused to help and would not be rushing to Cape Town; if their son needed an ambulance, it was his problem.

'I just saw red! I couldn't believe what I was hearing. This was my dearest friend's parents, and they couldn't have cared less if he lived or died. Or worse, if he was left brain damaged.' Maria immediately phoned her local Witness congregation and asked the elders for help. Could they please speak to her friend's parents? It was almost 11 p.m. at night, so she could not drive to the farm alone, but could someone perhaps drive with her?

Maria said that she was prepared to help in any way possible, but she needed the elders' help. 'I was promptly told not to get involved. The elders would call his parents and they would take it from there. I was told I was being too outspoken for my own good.' This display of patriarchal censure and cold dismissiveness was nothing new to Maria, but denying her request for help was the final straw. Her friend lay dying, for all she knew, alone and isolated from his family, and no one cared. Enough was enough!

'It was a huge snapping point for me. The bough had broken.' Maria lost all reason and argued furiously with her elders: 'I told them that if they didn't help my friend immediately, I would go to the press. With that kind of threat, and with me still in a state of public reproval, the conversation did not go down well at all.'

In the meantime, the young man's family had contacted the farm manager to say that they would not be able to come to the farm, but could they arrange with Maria for their son to be transported to Cape Town International Airport as soon as possible. They would fly from Johannesburg to meet Maria and their son there and then take him to Groote Schuur Hospital for examination.

Maria agreed, but by the time she was able to arrange the transport, the young man's family had already arrived in Cape Town and was en route to a nearby holiday home. They informed Maria that she would now need to bring him there.

'I was so upset and angry. I had driven all that way and there was no one to meet me at the airport. I went into the airport pharmacy and bought whatever epilepsy medicine I could find and then drove my friend to the holiday home and delivered him to his parents. They said they would take him to a doctor in Johannesburg after their holiday. Their apathy was incredible.'

That same week, Maria attended a family Bible-study session at Lara's house. Still angry at the previous days' events, Maria tried to relax by chatting and playing with her niece, who by now was almost three years old. 'We sat on the couch watching *Caleb and Sophia*, an in-house Jehovah's Witnesses children's cartoon. In it, a little girl, Sophia, stumbles across a coin on the ground in the park. She picks up the coin and dreams of buying the biggest ice cream ever. But, at that moment, Sophia's mother appears and wishes away the little girl's dream.

'She kneels beside Sophia and asks the little girl what would be the correct thing to do? "Buy an ice cream or give the money to the church?"'

Ironically, it was this 'innocent' cartoon dialogue, immersed in its own message of guilt and recrimination, that proved to draw the line in the sand that Maria needed: 'If ever one could feel both rage and numbness at the same time, that is what I felt at that exact moment.' Maria stood up from the couch, said goodbye to her niece and left her sister's house forever.

From that moment on, she ceased all Jehovah's Witnesses activities and informed her mother, sister and brother-in-law, the elder, that she intended to leave the church. Almost immediately, Lara stopped speaking to her, and Donna restricted her contact to the bare minimum. 'On 19 November 2019, I made an official announcement to my family that I was no longer a Jehovah's Witness – I was out! From that moment onwards, I was not able to associate with my mother or sister again.'

It was only two years later, on 5 March 2022, after the Covid-19 pandemic had swept across the globe, causing panic and pandemonium for the better part of 2020 and 2021, that Maria wrote a formal letter to her elders informing them that she was no longer a member of the Jehovah's Witnesses.

This is a copy of her letter:

> 5 March 2022
> To whom it may concern:
>
> I am writing this letter to the Jehovah's Witnesses' Organisation to inform you that I no longer want to be part of or associated with Jehovah's Witnesses!
>
> Please do not ever contact me nor send me religious articles going forward!
>
> Maria

With her decision to formally leave the Jehovah's Witnesses Church, Maria was officially disfellowshipped. After everything that had transpired and everything she had experienced, resolving to finally leave the church was a relatively easy decision to make. However, cutting all ties with her mother, sister and niece was one of the most challenging and saddest decisions of her life. During the course of Maria's departure from the Jehovah's Witnesses, she also received numerous threatening text messages: 'You bring reproach on Jehovah's name!'; 'You bring reproach on your family's name!' and 'Your movements on Facebook are being monitored and not taken lightly!'

Maria was no longer just 'shunned', she was now disfellowshipped, completely excommunicated from the church and, by default, her family. Shunning typically refers to the social isolation inflicted on an individual by one's Witness congregation for misdemeanours against the Witness faith, but provided the transgressor demonstrates repentance for their behaviour, they may be reinstated as a full member of their congregation. Disfellowshipping, on the other hand, is the harshest form of shunning and is typically a permanent, lifelong punishment, particularly if the individual does not show genuine repentance.

In some cases, if the individual is truly sorry for their sins, they may be allowed back into the fold, but it is a long and exhausting process. Although disfellowshipping is typically reserved for baptised Witnesses and is considered the ultimate punishment for someone who has previously sworn unconditional allegiance to Jehovah via their baptism, any Jehovah's Witness may be subjected to this fate if the elders deem it necessary.

For these individuals, as it was in Maria's case, leaving the faith is not just a process of losing their religion, but can also mean losing their loved ones. In many cases, friends and family are told to cut all ties with excommunicated Witnesses, leaving them isolated, completely ostracised and, in some instances, suicidal.

Her disfellowshipping took a huge toll on Maria's business: 'I also had to basically start my business again, as most, if not all, of my clients were Jehovah's Witnesses, and they withdrew or left.'

The act of disfellowshipping Witnesses, or apostates, as they are also commonly referred to, is a significant characteristic of the worldwide Jehovah's Witnesses congregation and is potentially also life-threatening, as attested to in a 2018 *Independent* article by a former elder from Poland:

> Those who leave the faith are called 'apostates' and are 'disfellowshipped', a term for formal expulsion and shunning, where members are 'prohibited from talking, and even from saying "hello" to them'. In one situation where an elder started to lose his faith and challenge the group, he said they allegedly denounced him and spread gossip about him, pressuring him 'so much he jumped into a river and killed himself'.

A related case tells the tragic story of Steven, the nephew of one of the Jehovah's Witnesses' most senior and prolific Governing Body members, Stephen Lett. As reported in the 2021 programme *Four Corners* on *ABC News In-depth*, in an episode titled 'Escaping Jehovah's Witnesses: Inside the Dangerous World of a Brutal Religion', Steven had admitted to his uncle and the rest of his family that he was gay. He was immediately shunned by both his congregation and his family. After five agonising years, Steven's sister secretly resumed contact with her brother, but the rest of the family continued to shun him, until he committed suicide in 2020.

Steven's disfellowshipping had caused him immense suffering and shame and resulted in his tragic end. He left the following instructions for his funeral: 'Things I don't want: the mention of religion or Jehovah's Witnesses upon my passing. They were the source of where this all began.'

Soon after Steven's death, Stephen Lett gave an online public address to the global Jehovah's Witnesses community in which he appears to mention his nephew and the lessons any Witness who strays from the path of righteousness should learn. In a disgraceful move, seemingly using Steven's death as a platform to 'teach' other Witnesses of the abomination of homosexuality and entrench anti-gay rhetoric, Lett claimed that with the imminent arrival of Armageddon, many who will be resurrected after the apocalypse will have to abandon their former way of life.

Lett explained that a young man he knew had been a homosexual but had since passed. However, at his resurrection, this young man would learn that Jehovah does not approve of homosexuality, and he would experience the true wrath of deviating from Jehovah's moral standards.

Jehovah's Witnesses rationalise disfellowshipping by claiming that although it causes much pain and suffering, it is, in fact, a 'loving provision' for both the evictee and the congregation alike. Two factors must coincide for the act of disfellowshipping to occur: first, a baptised Witness commits a serious sin; and second, he/she does not repent of his/her sin. JW.org says: 'Although Jehovah does not demand perfection from us, He does have a standard of holiness that He expects his servants to meet. For example, Jehovah insists that we avoid such serious sins as sexual immorality, idolatry, thievery, extortion, murder, and spiritism (1 Cor. 6:9, 10; Rev. 21:8).'

Jehovah's Witnesses argue that Jehovah has 'clean standards' and that these are reasonable and serve to protect all Witnesses. After all, according to JW.org: 'Who does not prefer to live among peaceful, decent people who can be trusted?' Thus, a 'servant of Jehovah' will be disfellowshipped if he or she commits a grave sin, if he or she is unrepentant and/or continues to practise that which is considered sinful. 'If genuine repentance is not manifest to the elders who serve on a judicial committee, they must disfellowship the person,' JW.org instructs.

Watchtower further explains that although the act of disfellowshipping may appear 'drastic or even unkind', Jehovah's teachings provide clear instruction that such a decision is, in fact, a loving one. Disfellowshipping is thus considered beneficial for everyone concerned. The JW.org website cites the following three benefits: disfellowshipping wrongdoers honours Jehovah's name; disfellowshipping protects the 'clean' Christian congregation; and disfellowshipping may bring the wrongdoer to his/her senses. While disfellowshipping is a spiritual tragedy, 'it need not become an unmitigated disaster as all of us play a role in making sure that the disfellowshipping serves its purpose'.

Jehovah's Witnesses claim that when the elders inform a Witness of their disfellowshipping, they go to great lengths to explain to that individual the steps they need to take to be reinstated in the congregation:

> To assist with their reinstatement, elders may, on occasions, visit and consult with the individual to assess any evidence of repentance. Family members can also show concern and love for their disfellowshipped relative as well as for their congregation by respecting the disfellowshipping decision, even if the disfellowshipped person is their son or daughter. As for the entire congregation, they too can show 'principled love' by avoiding all and any contact with the disfellowshipped person. The congregation thus reinforces the discipline that Jehovah has 'bestowed' them through the elders. – Romans 12:13, 15 (JW.org)

Jehovah's Witnesses do not engage in any spiritual or social fellowship with disfellowshipped Witnesses. A *Watchtower* article of 15 September 1981 explains why: 'A simple "Hello" to someone can be the first step that develops into a conversation and maybe even a friendship. Would we want to take that first step with a disfellowshipped person?' Strict avoidance is necessary, as a matter of loyalty to Jehovah and His Word: 'We obey Jehovah not only when it is convenient but also when doing so presents real challenges,' says JW.org.

If a relative is disfellowshipped and they still reside in the same household, Watchtower instructs that normal day-to-day family activities may continue, but those family members loyal to Jehovah may no longer have spiritual fellowship with the disfellowshipped person, as in when the family comes together for worship and prayer, or even for family meals. Only very limited conversation is allowed.

In the case where minor children have been disfellowshipped, their parents are still responsible for instructing and disciplining them. Where a relative is not living in the family home, the family should maintain only minimum contact with that person. In the words of JW.org: 'Loyal Christian family members do not look for excuses to have dealings with a disfellowshipped relative not living at home. Rather, loyalty to Jehovah and his organization moves them to uphold the Scriptural arrangement of disfellowshipping.'

For the most part, though, disfellowshipped family members, even young adults, are reportedly told to leave their homes and are barred from ever visiting them again. They are thus compelled to live with friends or even on the streets. A 2017 *BBC News* report describes the case of a young woman who was allegedly disfellowshipped for refusing to stay in an abusive relationship. Since involving the authorities in such matters is not exactly encouraged by the Jehovah's Witnesses organisation, her attempt to seek legal justice was punished by way of disfellowshipping and she was cut off from her family and friends.

In a statement, the Jehovah's Witnesses responded to the BBC: 'If a baptised Witness makes a practice of breaking the Bible's moral code, and does not give evidence of stopping the practice, he or she will be shunned or disfellowshipped.' On the night she was disfellowshipped, the young woman's mother apparently refused to talk to her, and by the following morning, her father had kicked her out of the family home. She was just twenty years old.

Responding to these claims, the Jehovah's Witnesses said that while it could not comment on individual cases, 'violence, whether physical or emotional, is strongly condemned in the Bible and has no place in a Christian family'.

In the two years since deciding to leave the Jehovah's Witnesses Church, in November 2019, and informing her family of her decision, to her formal 'resignation' to the elders in 2022, Maria still had a long way to go before she could call herself a former Witness and experience true freedom.

By January 2020, the world was grappling with a devastating global pandemic, Covid-19, which was fast making its way to the shores of South Africa. By March of that year, the country was forced into a national emergency lockdown. Maria still had to survive a pandemic…

CHAPTER 8

Good Things Come …

By the end of 2019, Maria found herself on the 'other side of the fence', and although the grass did appear a little greener, her business was struggling and needed a reboot. She was also slowly rebuilding her relationship with her father, but her sister wanted nothing to do with her. Maria's mother maintained minimal contact: 'My mom would visit me sometimes to "get her nails done". If it was just a business transaction, she was allowed to visit me. But I only did her nails for one month and then I stopped her visits because she gossiped, and she had strong opinions.'

The notable empty space in Maria's life, however, was a decent, loving companion, but it would take some time before she would truly be able to trust again. On 21 December 2019, Maria struck it lucky on an online dating application. We will call him Alex.

'By the 26th of December, we were chatting every day,' Maria recalls. 'The only snag was that he lived in Johannesburg, and I lived in Cape Town. He was only in Cape Town for the holidays. I told him I was not interested in a long-distance relationship, but he convinced me to at least give it a chance.'

For the next three months, Maria commuted between Cape Town and Johannesburg, and her relationship with Alex went from strength to strength. 'He was just the most amazing person – so kind, patient, funny – it was incredible. We were so compatible and so happy.' In the background, though, fears over the growing severity and spread of the Covid-19 virus began to take hold in South Africa.

The South African government eventually followed the rest of the world and declared a national state of disaster, with the country officially going into a nationwide lockdown from midnight on 26 March 2020. Unable to reschedule her flight back to Cape Town, Maria found herself stuck in Johannesburg and, for the foreseeable future, 'locked down' with Alex.

What initially appeared to be a minor catastrophe for Maria turned out to be the greatest blessing of her life. In those few weeks of Level 5 lockdown, with travel restrictions imposed, Maria and Alex fell deeper in love. Their fate was sealed. A new future for Maria – a brighter, truly happier one – lay before her. When travel restrictions were eased, Maria and Alex wasted no time in planning their future. On 26 December 2020, they were officially engaged, one year after meeting online.

Then, a few months later, in September 2021, Alex and Maria contracted Covid at the same time. Maria was hit hard and struggled to recover, but it was Alex who took a near-fatal turn. He was hospitalised with a high fever and breathing complications, and within a week was rushed into intensive care. It was a close call, with each day an anxious waiting game. Slowly, he turned the corner and began to recover. By the end of September, he was released from hospital but had a long recuperation ahead of him. Still, the young couple had everything to look forward to.

On 22 May 2022, Maria and Alex were married in a beautiful, intimate ceremony attended mostly by friends. There were few relatives, and, as Maria was, by now, officially disfellowshipped, there were no Jehovah's Witnesses ... bar one, a close friend of hers who, despite the Witnesses' rules, wanted to support the happy couple and celebrate with them. Maria says her friend 'has since started to question the Jehovah's Witnesses' doctrine and is slowly distancing himself from the organisation'.

The only family members to attend the ceremony were Maria's father and her half-brother, and, on Alex's side, his uncle and his uncle's family. Neither Alex's brothers nor his mother attended: 'Alex's mother and brothers refused to attend as I wasn't Jewish, and they are orthodox Jews.'

Despite the perfection of the day, Maria describes planning the actual wedding and honeymoon as 'stressful' because of the strict lockdown regulations and restrictions. 'Although everything went off so well at the wedding,' Maria remembers, 'we both got Covid again during our honeymoon. Friends arrived at our wedding already infected with the virus. Fortunately for us, though, it wasn't as bad the second time around.'

In our final interview for the book, Maria shared some deeply emotional and poignant life lessons that she hopes will not only convey a message of forgiveness and love, but also bring hope and encouragement to those members of the Witness community who may be struggling with their own convictions and harbouring doubts about the Kingdom of Jehovah.

Maria would like these individuals to know that there is a happy and fulfilling life outside the confines of the Jehovah's Witnesses Church, and that by rejecting their religious doctrines and unconditional dedication to a Governing Body of elders who claim to be servants of Jehovah, one does not necessarily have to turn one's back on God.

In Maria's words: 'Even though there are a lot of dark moments in life where you lose faith in religion and humanity, never stop believing in yourself and the happiness you can find, even when all hope seems lost. Never allow yourself to be lost in the pressures of life and the standards or rules of religion. Be balanced and follow your gut ... I truly feel that life shouldn't be so complicated and dictated by others ... Follow your hopes and dreams, whatever they may be, and never be afraid to be yourself. Sacrifices sometimes have to be made, but not in the way you think.

'Listen to your gut – it's usually right! Try to find your own belief system before following or being pushed into a religion that rules your entire being. Blood is not always thicker than water. Never stop believing in yourself and the things that you can accomplish.

'You can find happiness, and you deserve to be happy without having to prove anything to the religion you belong to. You are not judged by how many times you attend service and knock on doors.'

In Kyria Abrahams's book *I'm Perfect, You're Doomed*, she claims that she was continuously told that leaving the Jehovah's Witnesses 'would be like leaving the haunted cabin in the woods to go check on that strange noise. Never again would a disfellowshipped person find caring friends or experience true love, as these things did not exist in Satan's world.'

Of course, this is not the case in real life. It is not only possible to survive in a world beyond the gates of the Jehovah's Witnesses, but it is also possible to thrive, and Maria is testament to this. Establishing a life beyond the church requires an unconditional leap of faith: faith in oneself, in humanity and yes, if you like, in God too.

As Maria says: 'Extreme beliefs and rules only mean trouble. Stop believing the brainwashing they feed you. Life doesn't have to be so complicated and dictated by people that take religion to the extreme. You *will* find happiness; you are not going to be punished for the rest of your life if you choose to follow a different path. Family isn't everything if they are limiting your hopes and dreams. Stand up for yourself and broaden your horizons. Stop letting them control your mind.'

Of course, Maria has paid a huge price for her decision to renounce the Jehovah's Witnesses, having had to leave behind her mother, sister and niece. She is shunned, unwelcome, and potentially never able to communicate or spend time with them again. But, for her, the sacrifice has been worth it. Maria stands firm in her convictions and has this to say to Donna, Lara and the church she escaped: 'You don't own me and my life. You give life to a child to live their own dreams and to uplift them through the process. If birth meant a contract with terms and conditions, I don't think anyone would sign up for it.

'I'm not a failure or Satan's child because I turned down your rules and controlling ways. I deserve happiness just as much as anyone else, no matter what their rank is within a church. Stop judging and gossiping. And, on a more positive note, I hope the brainwashing gets washed away and may your eyes open to all the wonderful joys in this life.'

If Maria had her time over again, would she do things differently? What would she say to her younger self? 'I would listen to my gut from the start. I would try to find myself before I tried to find love. Never keep quiet and seek help immediately from people you can really trust and that have authority. I wouldn't have tried to please my mom and my sister before I pleased myself.

'Travel ... it opens your eyes to a broader horizon.

'I would not accept a fraction of the drama and demoralising behaviour that surrounded me.

'Enjoy the life you've been given. Make friends with people of all races and religions – you are no better than anyone else. May every second count and don't be afraid to live up to the standards you deserve. Forgive and move on without waiting for an apology; it only stifles you.

'Be kind and loving to the less fortunate. Don't always believe that people around you have your best interests at heart. Open your mind to all possibilities and start creating your own religion within nature ... it is the purest form of perfection. Always keep your heart and body safe – these are the only things you are born and die with.'

CHAPTER 9

Church or Cult?

'One person's religion is another person's cult.'

– Philip Seymour Hoffman

WHAT EXACTLY IS A CULT?

Loosely defined, a cult consists of a group of people who typically identify by their religious or spiritual beliefs, which are perceived as unusual or unorthodox because they practise a particular doctrine that appears to stray from what is considered the 'norm'. The term 'cult' tends to carry negative connotations because cult leaders are perceived as engaging in strange or exploitative behaviour in order to exercise pervasive control over their members, and their activities are often cloaked in secrecy.

'Cult' is a mystical word that apparently makes sense only to those on the outside, because those within the fold do not relate their experience to anything untoward, extreme or exploitative; in fact, cult members perceive it as quite the opposite, as these individuals find a deep sense of belonging and purpose within the cult. When an individual identifies with and wholeheartedly and unconditionally believes in the doctrine they are committed to, no matter how unusual it may be, they tend to feel completely 'enlightened' (and vilified by outsiders).

Unorthodox beliefs alone, however, do not necessarily a cult make, nor are they always ominous. There are more significant factors to consider: the leadership of the group, and the way leadership is enforced, are often more defining characteristics of a cult. A cult is typically led by a person (or a small group of people) who assumes a superior position of unquestionable authority over the cult's members.

Membership of the group is often sustained by coercion, manipulation, a distortion of the truth, false promises, fearmongering, and/or punishment at the hand of the leader or leaders. Another factor to consider is the origin of membership. Cult members are either born into the group or are actively recruited.

Recruiters are skilled at homing in on human tragedies or vulnerabilities that provide opportunity for infiltration. They tend to seek out individuals who have experienced recent trauma or loss and use these experiences first to console the person before 'marketing' the principles of their doctrine, providing just the right mix of solace and redemption. The individual who finds him- or herself in this vulnerable position may be so desperate to rid themselves of despair that they are easily swayed or manipulated by what the recruiter is offering and readily 'sign up' for just about anything.

As Steven Hassan writes in *Psychology Today*: 'If in a vulnerable state, you may fall for one of the many recruitment strategies. Some take place in person, where you may meet someone at work, through a friend or from a community. Or you may find yourself recruited online from social media posts, websites, YouTube videos, discussion forums, dating apps, movies or video games.'

Other key considerations in determining whether a cult is indeed a cult include the degree of appropriate influence over its members, which involves informed consent, the right to speak and question the rules and principles of membership, freedom to participate or leave the group without prejudice, and, most importantly, free will itself.

The leadership of a group considered to be a cult is likely to enforce inappropriate and unwarranted influence over its members, including discouraging and even punishing anyone who questions or speaks out against the group's rules and practices. They would typically use isolation tactics, coercion, fear and punishment, banishment, and even enslavement, as tools to control and entrap members. Leaders of a cult need to ensure that their members are tightly controlled, because where free will is at play, maintaining control over individuals becomes challenging, if not impossible.

They also need to find a balance between unquestionable loyalty and 'willing' obedience, as willingness is the key to a sustained, controlled membership. They therefore need to ensure that their members think they are willingly involved rather than being manipulated. Succeeding in this typically involves extreme yet subtle coercion and intimidation or overpromising a better future and/or a 'fantastical' afterlife. For many cult members, the institutionalised fear and dread of excommunication, even eternal damnation, is enough to ensure their compliance.

As Hassan explains in *Psychology Today*: 'When the mind is controlled, a victim may appear happy and willing to suffer for the profit or benefit of the leader/group. For members, happiness comes from "good" performance within the group, along with elitist thinking – believing they have the "truth" or the best way of life. But strict obedience is required. They are manipulated by fear and guilt and may be stuck, with no way out!'

By this definition, one could argue that almost any religious movement is a cult, and that 'religion' and 'cult' are potentially synonymous. In the scriptures of most Christian and many non-Christian-based faiths, there is a requisite compliance to 'divine' rules and principles (often outdated and outmoded in this new world order of feminism, political activism and equal rights movements). There are also threats of the 'end of days', plus the existence of a heaven and a hell with their promises of either a utopian afterlife or eternal life, or, conversely, threats of eternal damnation. Yet, the vast majority of these religious communities and their leaders would vehemently deny any similarity to a cult. 'Cult' is considered a dirty word that implies an ominous gathering of individuals who have abandoned all sane, rational thought and are presumably involved in profane, clandestine activities and have likely succumbed to total authoritarian leadership.

Take, for example, the case of Jim Jones, a radical preacher from Indianapolis in the United States, who, in November 1978, was responsible for the Jonestown massacre, the largest murder-suicide in American history. Jones preached a strange hybrid of gospel and Marxism to a racially well-integrated congregation. More than just a charismatic religious leader, he was a radical political activist and, seemingly, a paranoid narcissist.

Jones moved his church, the Peoples Temple, which numbered almost a thousand strong, from Indiana to northern California in search of a perfect, utopian community. This escapade was short-lived, however, as Jones faced pressure from his members' families, who demanded he set their relatives and children free and allow them to return home.

He also experienced one too many 'run-ins' with local law enforcement, forcing him to seek a new 'utopia' far away in the rainforests of Guyana in

South America. Their settlement was called Jonestown. Jones allegedly confiscated the members' passports and denied them communication or access to their families, all under the guise that their commune needed to remain secret for safety and security purposes.

Jones maintained control over his followers by way of false prophecies and promises, blackmail and a variety of punishments. When family members discovered the move to Guyana, they appealed to the US government for help. A delegation was sent to Jonestown, but it ended in a bloody confrontation when members of the delegation, including a few journalists and defectors from the Peoples Temple, were brutally attacked and shot as they attempted to flee the commune.

Immediately after the confrontation, Jones informed his followers that he could no longer protect them from the evil outside world, even though he had tried his best to give them a pure, utopian life. However, the events of that day had ruined their purpose on earth.

Within hours, on Jones's instruction, his followers committed mass suicide by drinking poison. As Jeff Guinn writes in his book *The Road to Jonestown: Jim Jones and Peoples Temple*: 'On that fatal day in November 1978, more than nine hundred people died including almost three hundred infants and children after being ordered to swallow a cyanide-laced drink.'

Jones took a quicker, easier route with a self-inflicted gunshot to the head.

In another case, a movement called Heaven's Gate, which became famous in the late 1990s for being a doomsday cult, committed mass suicide in 1997 to access what they believed would be an extraterrestrial spacecraft following the comet Hale-Bopp, which would be sent to save them from eternal damnation.

Although these 'end-of-days' prophecies are all too familiar in cult movements, they are not unique to so-called cults. 'End-of-days' predictions are also common in various established religious faiths, for example in Islam's Koran, which speaks of a 'judgement day', as well as the Bible's Book of Revelations in the New Testament, in which the events of 'the last days' are described.

For cult movements, though, doomsday predictions appear to have found a particularly useful home, as it is mostly effective as a means of intimidation and enforcing total control over their followers. If doomsday prophecies and 'end-of-days' predictions appear common to both traditional religions and cult movements, the lines between the two become blurred. How, then, do we differentiate a cult from a religion?

Determining a religious movement from a cult potentially involves a 'value judgement' based more on opinion and perception than fact. 'A cult is a group with a manipulative leader who financially exploits its members,' writes Suzanne Newcombe in her essay called 'Cults: History, Beliefs, Practices'. 'But by using this description, any group which tithes could be seen as a cult.'

In this context, then, relying on popular opinion also has its challenges, leading to a move in recent years to avoid the use of the word 'cult' in favour of the term 'new' or emergent religious movements and to researching and understanding their position in relation to modern society. Some of these 'new' religious movements are Christian-based, some have a very small following, and some practise a broad spectrum of beliefs and doctrines that appeal to different minorities and different age and social groups.

Some of these contemporary 'religions' do not even practise a religion in the traditional sense, favouring more holistic, mind-body healing practices and meditation. The recruitment of members may be internet-based and less aggressive, or it might be more proactive and coercive via face-to-face preaching strategies.

Whatever their approach, sociologists propose that while these new religions have characteristics that differentiate them from historically well-established religions and tend to exhibit more charismatic leadership and increasingly 'modernised' interpretations of age-old scriptures, possibly characterising them as more cult-like, they still identify as a religious movement and not as a cult. In fact, members of these emergent religions find the modern take on 'old-school' religious practices and teachings refreshing, relevant and progressive. And, over time, as members expand their families and their children practise the same religious principles as their parents, the membership grows organically rather than by cultish coercion or threat.

It could be argued that the distinguishing factor between a religion and a cult is the right to freedom of religion. Just as there should be no legal ground for governments to dictate an individual's right to practise or change their religion, so, too, should individuals have the right within their community and within their congregation to choose, change or renounce their faith without punishment or prejudice.

All citizens and community members should enjoy autonomy in their religious choices without criticism from fellow church members, members of the community and the legal system. In this context, freedom of religion becomes a key differentiator between cult and religion, including religious movements both new and old. Yet again, the term 'freedom of religion', as a distinguishing factor, is also problematic, particularly when one studies non-Christian-based faiths like Islam and Hinduism.

In many Islam-dominated countries, Muslims do not have the right to change their religion. They may even be sentenced to death on the grounds of renouncing or deserting their faith. In countries where Muslims are in the minority, as they are in Europe, the United States and Canada, they may take the law into their own hands, with family members exerting intense pressure on anyone wishing to leave the religion or going against its doctrine.

In some cases, disobeying one's father, traditionally the patriarchal head of the household, may even end in death. Consider the case of three Muslim sisters who were killed by their father in 2009 in Ontario, Canada, for bringing shame on the family.

Their father, an Afghan immigrant, was angered that his eldest daughter had gone against his wishes and married a Pakistani man. He believed that his two other daughters would bring similar shame on the family, and, as they had disrespected him, he felt it necessary to take the lives of all three, as well as their mother, in what is known as an 'honour killing', illegal under Canadian law and, importantly, also illegal in terms of the laws of Islam. This father, however, felt completely justified, as was reported in the *Daily Mail Online*.

Similarly, in India, where Hinduism is the dominant religion, many converts to Christianity have allegedly been forced to convert back to Hinduism, even under threat of death. What is most significant in both stories is that, despite the allegations, one would not consider either Islam or Hinduism a cult.

Generally, followers of a religious movement, both new and old, define themselves as believers or disciples and would be offended by the term 'cult member'. Tina Rodia, in an article penned for the University of

Pennsylvania's online press, *Penn Today*, writes that the word 'cult' is a term that should not refer to religion at all, but rather applies to a social movement. Take, for example, Mormonism and Scientology. Both are relatively new religious movements, dating from the nineteenth and twentieth centuries respectively, that have evolved into recognisable and established religions, yet research statistics reveal that non-Mormons in the United States are still likely to label Mormonism a cult.

According to the *Penn Today* article, 'Scientology and Mormonism have outlived their charismatic leaders. They have openly published their beliefs as scripture. Both religions seek truth by offering its followers a roadmap for their place in the universe, along with a moral code. Those who accept the beliefs and rituals are members of the religion. But many outside consider the movement, and its followers, to be a cult. How have the two been conflated?'

New religious movements are not necessarily cult-like; many have evolved since the nineteenth century, where global cyclical economic depression, increasing socio-economic woes, and a growing dissatisfaction and disillusionment with centuries-old versions of Christianity have driven a quest for something new and contemporary that represents a fresh perspective on traditional, yet outmoded, scriptures and provides a modern take on prayer and worship.

The *Penn Today* article states that 'People [in Western communities] were disillusioned with Christianity and moved to the suburbs and became more secular. In the mid-20th century, people left their birth communities, or lost touch with their original congregations and looked for more modern worship.'

Under these circumstances, there has been a sharp global increase in new religious movements and charismatic churches, particularly in the past seventy to eighty years. These conditions have also been perfect for the birth of non-Christian movements like Scientology and the Hare Krishnas.

For every action there is a reaction, however, and, with time, anti-cult movements also emerged, fusing the term 'cult' with any fringe movement outside of what is considered an established traditional religion, which feeds the discord in consensus around what is deemed a cult and what is deemed a recognised religion.

The *Penn Today* article contends that the distinction between religion and cult becomes even more complex when one considers the following two criteria: firstly, leadership style: 'Religions and cults often follow a leader who claims divine, or at least special access to different models of knowledge and revelations. Many are martyred. Jesus of Nazareth was famously crucified. Joseph Smith, Mormonism's founder, was lynched'; and, secondly, the prophecies of the 'end of days': 'End days is another consistent theme in both cults and religions, both new and old. Nirvana, heaven, Zion, or outer space are all a guiding principle in their scriptures.'

Perhaps one factor that could differentiate between a cult and a religion is time. Scientology is now recognised in the US as a religion, with a similar tax-exempt status to the Jehovah's Witnesses. And, although Mormonism was considered 'such a deviant form of heterodoxy that its founder was lynched', the Mormon Church today is also a recognised religion with more than 14 million members worldwide, according to the *Penn Today* article.

It could be that surviving the course of time with sufficient members intact provides the elevation from cult status to bona fide religion. 'As long as there is orthodoxy, there will be heterodoxy,' claims the *Penn Today* article, 'and there will continue to be gospels of the end of days that are rooted in science or scripture, people seeking answers, and leaders emerging who claim to have them. Whether their followers are cult members or parishioners will largely be a matter of time.'

Defining a cult is thus not as straightforward as one might think. It is a multifaceted, controversial and personally emotive dynamic. The term 'cult' has acquired a villainous, sometimes scandalous, reputation that seems to prey on the very attributes that define us as human beings: our need for purpose, our need to belong and our desire to find meaning in life, be it on this mortal coil or beyond.

Because of their typical demand for unconditional and unquestioning dedication to often misplaced dogma, some of which are irrational and even dangerous, cults carry ominous connotations. Not all apocalyptic religious movements are necessarily cults, however, and not all cults, like the Peoples Temple or Heaven's Gate, end in mass suicide or wait expectantly for spaceships to rescue them.

The Seventh-day Adventists, for example, which emerged from the

Adventist movement that swept through the United States during the 1840s and predicted a catastrophic end to human existence in 1843 (based on their calculations – or, rather, miscalculations – from the Book of Daniel) may have surged ahead of themselves only to end up dispersing into splinter groups when one prophecy after another failed to materialise. Yet they managed to reorganise themselves into new religious movements, some of which progressed and survive to this day.

One such movement was the International Bible Students Association, known today as the Jehovah's Witnesses. The Seventh-day Adventists have themselves grown into a global congregation represented in over 200 countries with a membership of more than 14 million. To this end, the question remains whether the Jehovah's Witnesses are a religion or a cult. Even though they continue to prepare for an imminent Armageddon, is it fair to label them a cult? Let us consider some of the facts …

Jehovah's Witnesses have often been accused of rewriting and distorting original Bible verses to validate and enforce their own version of the Bible, thus misrepresenting original scriptures of Christianity. Jehovah's Witnesses vehemently refute this allegation and claim that everything they do is strictly in the name of Jehovah, and that the end of days is a real and imminent event in the Christian calendar.

The fundamental practices of their religion, however, including their version of Armageddon and the practice of disfellowshipping, stand in stark contrast to traditional teachings of mainstream Christianity and, arguably, serve to control members by way of shaming, reproving, shunning and threatening them with exclusion from the Kingdom of Jehovah after Armageddon.

Although their public-relations campaign projects an image of modest living within a benign, conservative milieu of loving worship to Jehovah God, with mostly law-abiding behaviour (bar the alleged sex-abuse cover-ups and the many reported underage disfellowships), it seems, on the flipside, that there is also evidence of manipulation, coercion and even brainwashing to ensure that its members succumb to a life of absolute submission to irrational rules and illogical, oppressive practices. Attempts to question these practices, not least the logic of the two-witness rule, can result in shaming and shunning, if not outright disfellowshipping.

While many consider the Jehovah's Witnesses a branch of Christianity, those who have been members of this community might argue to the contrary. Rewriting their interpretation of the Bible, preparing for Armageddon or protesting blood transfusions do not in themselves make the Jehovah's Witnesses a cult, nor do their misogynistic and anti-gay sentiments. Even the scandal of alleged sexual abuse is not unique to the Jehovah's Witnesses.

Rather, it is the practice of shunning and disfellowshipping that is a cause for concern and one that is unique to the Witness congregation. No matter the age of a member, be it a teenager or an adult, if the individual strays from the pack, disregards the rules or chooses not to be a Witness any more, the practice of disfellowshipping casts a dark shadow over the Witnesses' capacity for compassion, tolerance and forgiveness.

As mentioned, disfellowshipping requires a family to cut all ties with the straying individual, even if he or she is still a teenager, and, in effect, to treat them as if they are dead. Being cut off from one's family and friends and the only community one knows can cause extreme anxiety and distress, and even result in suicide. In any community, families should be able to engage with each other regardless of faith or religion.

Jehovah's Witnesses claim that they are not a cult. In the words of JW.org: 'We are Christians who do our best to follow the example set by Jesus Christ and to live by his teachings.' The Jehovah's Witnesses' official website dedicates a special page to an explanation of what a cult is and why it is not a cult: 'The term "cult" means different things to different people. However, consider two common perceptions regarding cults and why those perceptions don't apply to us:

'**Some think of a cult as being a new or unorthodox religion.** Jehovah's Witnesses have not invented a new religion. On the contrary, we pattern our worship after that of the first-century Christians, whose example and teachings were recorded in the Bible (2 Timothy 3:16, 17). We believe that the Holy Scriptures should be the authority on what is orthodox in matters of worship.

'**Some think of a cult as being a dangerous religious sect with a human leader.** Jehovah's Witnesses do not look to any human as their leader. Rather, we adhere to the standard that Jesus set for his followers when he stated: "Your Leader is one, the Christ" (Matthew 23:10).'

Rather than a dangerous cult, they profess to be a Christian-based religion that is founded on the principles of compassion, concern, impartiality and altruism, with their one true leader, Jehovah God. Again, the public-relations cogs turn smoothly; it is a well-oiled machine. Their website righteously justifies their practice of disfellowshipping, their aversion to higher education, their subjugation of women and the closely guarded activities of their male-only 'Governing Body', not to mention the gross neglect and concealment of alleged sexual abuses within their ranks. Again, one can argue that many of these features are not too dissimilar to those of other traditionally recognised religions.

The Catholic Church, for example, also defers to a tightly knit band of senior 'elders' or cardinals, who surround and support their leader, the Pope, of which there has never been a female cardinal or a female Pope. The Catholics have also endured wave upon wave of allegations regarding decades-long suppression of rampant child sex abuse within their ranks. Yet, even within this context, the Catholic Church is hardly referred to as a cult. By association, then, is it plausible that the Jehovah's Witnesses Church is a cult?

To answer this question, one needs to review, in more detail, the basic tenets of the Jehovah's Witnesses. In addition to the practice of disfellowshipping (already discussed), another area of concern is the issue of accurate Bible translation. In trying to understand exactly how the Watch Tower Society came to write their own version of the Bible, one removes the veil of piety to expose something that might seem a little more menacing.

Jehovah's Witnesses claim to have the most accurate translation of the Bible, known as the 'New World Translation'. This translation is a version of the Bible that was created by the Watch Tower Society and allegedly contains subtle but deceptive changes to many Bible verses. Jehovah's Witnesses are instructed to only read the New World Translation of the Bible and not any other version (including the New King James Version or the English Standard Version), as they are told that every other version is inaccurate except for their own.

It is critical to note that the original version of the Old Testament was written in Hebrew, while the New Testament portion of the Bible was originally written in a dialect of Greek known as Koine Greek (the reason being that Greek was the dominant written and spoken language of the eastern Mediterranean region when Rome was the ruling empire during the New Testament period).

To accurately and directly translate the original New Testament portion of the Bible into English would therefore require a considerable knowledge of ancient Greek. The Watch Tower Society released their translation of the New Testament portion of the Bible in 1950; it is known as the New World Translation of the Christian Greek Scriptures. The complete rendition of the New World Translation of the Bible, which includes the Old Testament, was released in 1961.

In his book, *'Knock Knock' Who's There? 'The Truth' About Jehovah's Witnesses*, former Jehovah's Witness Anthony James claims that the Watch Tower Society has repeatedly raised concern for misquoting numerous notable scholars, often in a way that shows biased support for their New World Translation. In addition to criticism lodged against those passages that demonstrate unsubstantiated bias towards Watchtower's doctrines, the original translators of the New World edition have also come under scrutiny, particularly because their identities and the credentials required to translate and write the New World Translation have remained unknown for decades. It was claimed that their names were never published for reasons of humility. Anthony James reveals the following:

> Raymond Franz was the nephew of the president of the Watchtower Society Fred Franz. He served as a member of the Governing Body for nine of his sixty years serving as a Jehovah's Witness. After being conspired against and removed from office and later the religion entirely, he wrote and published one of the best exposés ever produced on Jehovah's Witnesses. The book *Crisis of Conscience* (1983) explains that of the four men who made up the translation team, only his uncle Fred Franz had any training in Greek. He had studied it for two years and was only self-taught in Hebrew. Interestingly, in a court case, Fred Franz was asked to translate a simple passage from the Bible (Genesis 2:4). He refused, stating, 'No I wouldn't attempt to do that.' Quite how this clearly incompetent team managed to translate the whole Bible, remains to be explained.

In addition to their practice of disfellowshipping and their dubious translation of the Bible, there remains the contentious issue of Armageddon, specifically the 'bizarrely' numbered 144 000 deserving souls who will be delivered safely to heaven while the rest of the Jehovah's Witnesses (and potentially the rest of humankind) will either be allowed to enter an earthly paradise or be forever obliterated.

How Jehovah God and his Witnesses arrived at this peculiar number of 144 000 is, quite possibly, a strong indicator of cult-like characteristics. Not to mention the practice of shunning birthdays and holidays, having zero tolerance for homosexuality, as well as the numerous heartfelt testimonies of former Witnesses who speak of psychological abuse, religious hypocrisy and sexual exploitation, which all point towards cult-like behaviour.

AND WHAT ABOUT BRAINWASHING?

Research on thought reform and mind-control techniques, conducted by American psychiatrist Robert Lifton in the 1950s, revealed the methods the Chinese government had employed during the Korean War to convince captured American pilots to embrace communist ideology. Lifton's research provided the basis from which techniques to debrief former cult members evolved.

Lifton identified eight thought-reform practices that form a framework from which to classify which religions use coercion and manipulation to control their members. These eight practices are summarised as follows:

> Milieu Control: the control of information to which a member is exposed leading to degrees of social isolation; Mystical Manipulation: a manipulation of events by the group's leadership to demonstrate 'divine' authority; Demand for Purity: members are required to conform unconditionally to the ideology of the group, often using guilt or shaming techniques; Confession: sins, as defined by the group's leadership, are to be confessed publicly or to a personal elder and then either exploited or punished by the leaders; Sacred Science: the group's doctrine is superior to all other doctrines and beyond reproach as is the leader of the group who is typically just a vessel through which God communicates; Loading

> the Language: the group typically has its own jargon and use of language that differs [from] the outside world, creating a secular sense of conformity to the group; Doctrine Over Person: no one member or their needs is more important than the overarching doctrine of the group; Dispensing of Existence: the group has the divine power to decide who is saveable and who is doomed, and labelling those outside of the group as unenlightened and only saveable if they convert to the group's ideology. If they do not conform to the group or are critical of the group, then they must be spurned by the members. In addition, any member who willingly leaves the group, must also be shunned.

Taking Lifton's eight principles into consideration, there are several similarities one can draw with the Jehovah's Witnesses. For example: the Governing Body, by way of the Watch Tower Society, controls the flow of information by enforcing strict adherence to their version of the Bible and disallowing consultation with any other version, as well as discouraging higher education among its congregation (Milieu Control); the practice of shunning and disfellowshipping and the threat of eternal damnation (Demand for Purity and Dispensing of Existence); the decisions and instructions of the Governing Body are beyond reproach and are not to be questioned, as they are not considered the head of the Jehovah's Witnesses, merely the messengers of Jehovah, their one true God.

Watchtower's doctrine rationalises that it is Jehovah who guides and directs the Governing Body of the Watch Tower Society and that its members are merely his faithful servants, and that Jehovah is the only true God (Sacred Science); to survive Armageddon, Jehovah's Witnesses must separate themselves from the outside world and follow the divine rules of the Watch Tower Society as decreed by Jehovah God. Failure to do so is deserving of disfellowshipping and, ultimately, exclusion from the Kingdom of Heaven.

Members must therefore conform unconditionally or face punishment if they digress or leave (Demand for Purity and Dispensing of Existence); members who commit a sin are expected to appear before a tribunal of elders to publicly confess their sin and await punishment. Victims of sexual abuse are required to do the same, even 'confessing' their potential 'part' in their abuse, often in front of their abuser. And, without a second witness to their abuse, their claims are considered invalid (Confession).

Steven Hassan, an American cult specialist and author of *Combating Cult Mind Control*, developed the BITE model, which attempts to explain the issue of cult-member-control across four categories. Hassan believes that a group becomes 'unhealthy' if it uses specific measures of control to keep followers dependent and obedient.

The first category relates to behavioural control, which includes the manipulation of one's physical environment by demanding an unreasonable amount of time for group meetings, activities and missionary work, as well as obedience to uncompromising rules that relate to appearance, entertainment, education and moral behaviour.

As James writes in *'Knock Knock' Who's There? 'The Truth' About Jehovah's Witnesses*: 'While Witnesses are not segregated physically from the rest of the world, they are to remain separate spiritually. Unnecessary association with "worldly" people is very much frowned upon and can even lead to an individual being "marked" themselves as bad association. Former members must be shunned and treated as though they do not even exist.'

Witnesses are expected to attend every weekly meeting, every Sunday church service and daily Bible-study sessions and do as much door-to-door missionary work as possible, with a minimum of ten hours per month. Individualism is discouraged, and a strict, conservative dress code for both men and women is enforced. Men are also not allowed facial hair (no beards or moustaches) and women have to wear skirts below the knee and evince modest fashion, make-up and jewellery choices.

Tertiary education is completely shunned, as Witnesses should rely on the Watch Tower Society for all the spiritual education that they need to guide them in their lives. Watchtower also claims that since Armageddon is imminent, it is a waste of time to over-educate oneself, only to be resurrected into a new paradise where 'worldly' education would be redundant.

The second category relates to information control, where information that is disseminated to the membership is controlled by the leadership and may be withheld, distorted or falsified as necessary – a form of propaganda indoctrination, in other words. The pursuit of knowledge other than that prescribed by the leadership is greatly discouraged or even outlawed, especially if it contradicts the teachings of the leadership or is critical of its practices.

James claims the following in his book: 'Secular sources may be used to back up the claims and teachings of the Watchtower, but they can never be viewed as reliable. After all, they are the work of imperfect and fallible men. Anything that is critical of the Watchtower Society, or the teachings of Jehovah's Witnesses is to be avoided, especially that of former members (Apostates).'

And he quotes the following from *The Watchtower*, 1 June 1967, page 338: 'In Jehovah's organization it is not necessary to spend a lot of time and energy in research, for there are brothers in the organization who are assigned to that very thing.'

The third category is thought control, whereby the group's doctrine must be internalised as the only 'truth', without question. Simple categorising, like 'good and evil' or 'us and them', is encouraged. In *'Knock Knock' Who's There?*, Anthony James purports that 'Almost ironically, a term that is without doubt the most commonly used phrase by Jehovah's Witnesses is "The Truth". I must insist you look at the fact that this expression works on the subconscious level of believers and its ready and frequent use "hardwires" it into the mind.

'As a Witness lives his or her life, this acts as a constant reminder that they are in "the truth", part of "the truth", and working for "the truth". This is not only present in the mind; it is persistent, and deeply burrowed. It is for these reasons I call it a textbook mind control or brainwashing technique.'

James claims that, in Watchtower's literature, there is no room for doubt that the Watch Tower Society is anything other than God's chosen messenger, and no other belief system that can be viewed as legitimate, good or useful. The Watch Tower Society is constantly challenged to keep undermining any alternative belief system in order to uphold their own, as seen in this extract from James's book:

> Do we hear valueless things being uttered today? Yes. For example, some scientists say that evolutionary theory and scientific discoveries in other fields demonstrate that there is no longer any need to believe in God,

> that everything can be explained by natural processes. Should such proud statements concern us? Of course not! Human wisdom differs from divine wisdom (1 Cor. 2:6, 7). However, we know that when human teachings contradict what God has revealed, it is always the human teachings that are wrong. (Read Romans 3:4.) Despite the progress of science in some fields, the Bible's assessment of human wisdom remains true: 'The wisdom of this world is foolishness with God.' Compared with the infinite wisdom of God, human reasoning is futile. – 1 Cor. 3:18-20

The last category is environmental control, which attempts to exploit an individual's natural tendency to harbour feelings of angst or fear in order to control their behaviour and strengthen their commitment to the group. In terms of the Jehovah's Witnesses, this includes encouraging a fear of 'worldly people', of being shunned and disfellowshipped, and of being rejected from eternal salvation.

Most importantly, an individual under mind control cannot contemplate or rationalise an alternative future outside of the group that is hopeful and positive. Hassan believes that the most important consideration when differentiating a religion from a cult is how members who wish to leave, or have left the group, are treated. The Jehovah's Witnesses enforce a strict shunning process on those who leave, and an even worse shunning for those who are formally disfellowshipped. Loyalty is always, first and foremost, to Jehovah God:

> What if we have a relative or a close friend who is disfellowshipped? Now our loyalty is on the line, not to that person, but to God. Jehovah is watching us to see whether we will abide by his command not to have contact with anyone who is disfellowshipped.
>
> – *The Watchtower*, 15 April 2012, page 12

CONCLUDING COMMENTS

Jehovah's Witnesses have a strong sense of community and appear to embrace a disciplined yet loving way of life, with the promise of eternal paradise for all those who follow the way of Jehovah. It is a seemingly benign religious movement that appeals to a substantial number of followers, or why else would they enjoy a membership of 8 million people worldwide?

Yet many former Witnesses refer to the Watch Tower Society as a fear-based doomsday cult that considers itself above all other belief systems, pious and superior, controlling and unrelenting. It seems that its membership is managed and retained mostly by way of information control and manipulation, which extends beyond the shunning of higher education and the enforced use of their own version of the Bible, to morally questionable leadership that enables child and adult sex abuse, seemingly condones the two-witness rule and the under-reporting of sexual abuse, and allegedly forces wives to remain with their violent husbands, all under the threat of being disfellowshipped.

These are not the practices of a loving, compassionate religion, regardless of how well established the church may be or how many followers it represents. Some might argue that their beliefs seem unorthodox and that their rules are too strict or too extreme, but Witnesses claim to have rational and logical reasons for everything they say and do.

For active Witnesses, there is nothing strange about their personal doctrine, which echoes the sentiments of many non-Witness religious leaders who believe that all religions have their own belief systems, rules and regulations. Jehovah's Witnesses, therefore, should not be viewed as a bizarre cult, but as a recognised religion with a specific belief system that is grounded in the Bible and enforced by its own internal measures of discipline.

Consider the story, covered by *USA Today*, of a recent murder-suicide in Michigan, United States, where a former Jehovah's Witness, a young mother of two, killed her husband and her two young children before turning the gun on herself, claiming that the family had been so badly ostracised by their Witness community when they decided to leave the church that the only way to save themselves from all the hurt and pain, and from future condemnation, was to kill them.

Jehovah's Witnesses, however, claim that disfellowshipping is a 'loving' practice, engineered only to make former Witnesses feel so isolated that they realise the error of their ways and return to the faith and the 'loving' fold of Jehovah. For this young family, however, it was not the case.

In a stunning headline on *CNN World News Online* on 10 March 2023

– 'Deadly Mass Shooting at Jehovah's Witnesses Center in Hamburg Stuns Germany' – a former Witness gunned down six people, and an unborn child, at a Jehovah's Witnesses centre in Hamburg, Germany, before turning the gun on himself. The mother of the unborn child survived her injuries. The gunman acted alone. Four men and two women between the ages of thirty-three and sixty died in the attack, and a further eight people were wounded. None of the victims were related to the shooter.

The gunman had reportedly left the Jehovah's Witnesses Church on bad terms eighteen months prior to the shooting. It was not yet clear if he had been disfellowshipped or had left voluntarily. Police had ruled out political motive or terrorism, citing possible mental illness. At the time of printing this book, the motive for the crime has not been established, but it is not too far-fetched to assume that the shooter was extremely upset with his former congregation and wanted retribution.

As mentioned, Jehovah's Witnesses claim that the practice of disfellowshipping is an act of love, intended only to show others how they have erred and to facilitate their return to the faith with even greater enlightenment. The reality, however, is that with its numerous tragic consequences, disfellowshipping is quite possibly the harshest method of mind control within the Jehovah's Witnesses' arsenal of manipulation tactics.

So, are the Jehovah's Witnesses a cult? Former Witness and author Anthony James will tell you: 'Without a doubt!' Maria's father, Albert, will tell you: 'They're a bunch of hypocrites, concerned only with indoctrination to control your thoughts and your life.' Certainly, Maria will tell you: 'I feel they are a cult of some form and lives have been destroyed because of them.'

Cult or religion, when it comes to the Jehovah's Witnesses, it is not actually a distinction that warrants too much dissection. What really matters is the fact that, for the many thousands of former Witnesses who have taken the bold step to leave the faith and, by default, their families, there is the undeniable shared sense of relief of having freed themselves from the shackles of an overbearing, over-controlling, sometimes ridiculous but, certainly, in their experience, a loveless church. As Daniel Clark writes in *I, Witness: The Shocking Insider's Story of Jehovah's Witnesses*:

I once called myself a Jehovah's Witness through and through. I was wrong. I was never a Jehovah's Witness. I was always and simply a child of God. When I put aside the colourful little Watchtower guides and read the scriptures on my own, when I remove the intermediaries between me and God, I see that His message as delivered through Christ is not about blood transfusions or voting, celebrating holidays or birthdays, or preparing for the end of the world by withdrawing from it. It is about love. As I grow, I learn even more about how to love, not just my wife and children and my extended and spiritual families, but my fellow human beings everywhere.

CHAPTER 10

Conclusion

The enigma that is the Jehovah's Witnesses endures. The beliefs and practices of this church have attracted decades-long scrutiny and criticism: it has been opposed by governments, religious groups and local communities alike, with many Christian-based faiths labelling them heretics, and even classifying them as a cult.

For the many Jehovah's Witnesses who have left the religion, there are few positives. Like Maria, they speak of childhoods consumed by Bible-study sessions, relentless meetings at Kingdom Hall, door-to-door missionary work, no birthday or holiday celebrations, no sport or social activities outside of the church, few to no friends outside of their congregation, haunting images of an ever-imminent Armageddon and, most disturbing of all, the constant threat of disfellowshipping.

Then there is also the dubious indoctrination of higher education being considered both unnecessary and a bad influence. Why pursue an education in the worldly system when the best education can be found within the Jehovah's Witnesses Church? A Witness was quoted as saying the following on the 2021 *ABC News* programme: 'We will not need doctors and lawyers after Armageddon, only carpenters and plumbers to maintain an earthly paradise.'

The Jehovah's Witnesses have incorrectly predicted the advent of Armageddon four times, which makes it doubly ironic that the Watch Tower Society is so heavily invested in various long-term property portfolios. Their headquarters are located in one of the most prime real-estate areas of upstate New York, while their extensive and lucrative property investments around the world house their numerous Bethels and Kingdom Halls. If Armageddon is imminent and it is considered a waste of time to invest in a tertiary education, what, then, is the rationale behind their extensive real-estate portfolio?

The disturbing allegations of widespread sexual abuse and the under-reporting of such abuse also makes one question the credibility, authenticity and morality of the Jehovah's Witnesses. This, in addition to their apparent condemnation of homosexuality. As a former Witness, who is gay, joked on the *ABC News* programme: 'Individuals are told they must just pray the gay away!'

Jehovah's Witnesses are taught from a young age that the world outside of their close-knit community is an evil place populated by 'worldly' people who are all part of the Devil's system. Leaving Jehovah's fold would most certainly thrust any Witness into a world of danger, corruption and evil temptation. And to find oneself outside of Jehovah's gate when Armageddon strikes would be the most damning of all.

Witnesses are taught that when the 'final days' arrive, only the most faithful will be automatically saved, while everyone else will die a horrible death. And because of this, to minimise the bloodshed and to keep their hands clean of blood, it is every Witness's responsibility to convert as many people as possible in the time left on this earth.

The pressure to save humankind from untold suffering and carnage is an unrelenting challenge for every committed Witness. For many of them, it is an anxiety-provoking, even soul-destroying, process, but for others it becomes a source of deeply ingrained security and comfort, even a sense of superiority, knowing that they have 'a safe passage to eternal life'.

The practice of disfellowshipping provides an effective means of maintaining strict adherence to the rules and requirements of the Witness church. The fear of being excommunicated and removed from one's family, friends and community, and the only way of life one has ever known, provides a cruel yet 'absolute' deterrent to disobedience. Disfellowshipping is supposedly practised only as a way of teaching Witnesses the lessons of non-compliance while trusting that they will repent and come back into the fold. But for those who have been forced out of their home and sent into a world they do not know, it is not just a frightening lesson but a cruel and unjustifiable outcome. For some, it spells a tragic end.

The many contradictions spoil the well-manicured facade of the Jehovah's Witnesses Church, but none is more damaging or disturbing than the scale of the alleged sexual-exploitation and child sex-abuse claims that have gone unchecked and under-reported for decades.

The damning 2016 landmark report by the Australian Royal Commission provides evidence of these allegations. In the report, the Jehovah's Witnesses in Australia are slated for not reporting or addressing abuse allegations that date back many years, but instead hiding behind their self-imposed two-witness rule to mitigate circumstances.

The Royal Commission recommended that the organisation elect women to their in-house judicial committees, abandon their two-witness rule and stop shunning those who have left because of abuse. However, the church refused to take these recommendations on board, citing only that their practices are based on the Bible. However, they have since confirmed that they will comply with the request to report abuse claims to legal authorities, although they have instructed their congregations that even though it is a Witness's right to report any allegation to the police, it is not a requirement, thus placing the onus back on the Witness community. With the ever-present threat of shunning and disfellowshipping, who is likely to report anything?

While the Royal Commission successfully resolved over 900 claims of abuse across various denominations listed in their report, not one of these cases related to those against the Jehovah's Witnesses. As reported on the *ABC News* programme, the Australian branch of the Jehovah's Witnesses stated that there was no evidence that they had acted inappropriately, and that they were not guilty of institutional abuse.

Testimony after testimony on the JW.org official website reveals a hard-working, peace-loving, religious community that identifies with the principles of Christianity, their sole purpose being Bible education for all. They deny that they are a cult and do not consider themselves 'unorthodox heretics'; rather, they identify as human beings with the same joys and challenges as everyone else, desiring only to serve Jehovah God:

> In most ways Jehovah's Witnesses are like everyone else. They have normal problems – economic, physical, emotional. They make mistakes at times, for they are not perfect, inspired, or infallible. But they try to learn from their experiences and diligently study the Bible to make needed corrections. They have made a dedication to God to do his will, and they apply themselves to fulfil this dedication. In all their activities they seek guidance from God's Word and his holy spirit.

Shining the spotlight on South Africa, the local Jehovah's Witnesses lay claim to extensive charitable community work that they believe reflects their selfless compassion and dedicated commitment to Jehovah God, their brothers and sisters, and their broader communities.

During the heavy rainfalls of April 2022, when KwaZulu-Natal and its many residents were hard hit by flash floods and mudslides, resulting in widespread loss of life and devastating damage to property, the Witness community came to the rescue. Many areas were without electricity or water for days and countless roads were washed away. Local Kingdom Halls opened their doors to offer disaster relief, shelter and food, and not just to their own Witness brothers and sisters, but also to the wider communities.

The Jehovah's Witnesses in South Africa have also been praised for their contribution to the deaf community of South Africa. Campaigners for the deaf community have thanked the Jehovah's Witnesses for helping hearing-impaired people to improve their lives by providing high-quality Bible materials in South African Sign Language (SASL). According to JW.org: 'The deaf and hard of hearing deserve a Bible in their language. That is why we commend Jehovah's Witnesses for providing Bible books to the deaf community in the language of their heart. We can't wait to have all the 66 Bible books in sign language.'

In 2023, on JW.org, a Canadian-born Witness, who spent over forty years in South Africa working as a printing-press technician, missionary and pioneer before returning to the US to join a branch committee of the Jehovah's Witnesses, described his life in South Africa with the Jehovah's Witnesses Church as an awe-inspiring, spiritual journey. Because of the Jehovah's Witnesses' faith and way of life, he claims that his life has been the 'ultimate' in emotional fulfilment and that it was a true privilege to serve Jehovah and His Witnesses.

Another posting, by a local South African Witness, expresses similar sentiments. He describes how the Jehovah's Witnesses organisation has grown since the early days, when he served in their local Cape Town branch office in a small congregation of seventeen Witnesses. They did not have a Bethel home initially, but grew into an extended congregation of over 460 who reside in a modern Bethel complex with sophisticated technology and rotary presses, which they now call home:

> Yes, I have had the privilege of growing up with Jehovah's organization in South Africa. I thank Jehovah that I have, for the past 40 years, had such a supportive wife at my side. 'My cup is well filled.' (Psalm 23:5) My wife and I are grateful to be part of Jehovah's spirit-directed organization and are determined to continue serving Jehovah in his house, in Bethel, and to keep up with his forward-moving organization.

For the many thousand positive declarations by Jehovah's Witnesses around the world, there are thousands more that attest to a different reality, one that is oppressive, restrictive and authoritarian, if not outright abusive. Maria's story is one such testimony: 'Every day was a constant struggle, even now. I fear going to the shops or events and seeing anyone who is related to the church, seeing them preaching and always being treated so badly. I have to keep my anxiety at bay the entire time because of what I have been through.

'I will hopefully get to a place in my life where it is a distant memory and that it no longer affects me. I will never entertain the Jehovah's Witnesses at my door, nor will I ever be in contact with anyone that believes in that religion ever again. I feel they are a cult of some form and lives have been destroyed because of it.'

No longer holding back, and no longer waiting for 'an eternal earthly paradise', Maria has created her own paradise, right here, today, on earth, with a thriving career and a loving new family. Time and again she taught herself to survive, through years of reproval and alienation. During protracted episodes of anxiety and despair, she could find rest only by taking strong sleeping pills. She coped, alone, with the loss of her baby girl, as well as the horror of sexual abuse at the hands of her fiancé, a fellow Witness. Then there was the emotional abuse the elders inflicted on her when she had to relive that ordeal and accept culpability in her own rape.

But Maria chose to keep moving forward, towards a more meaningful and less restrictive life, and, in the end, she succeeded. Despite the despair and the many sacrifices she made along the way, none more so than being excommunicated by her mother and sister, Maria has discovered a new 'truth': that there is a world beyond the walls of the church where genuine love and kindness reside, where she no longer has to be alone, shunned or condemned.

At the time of publishing this book, Maria remains happily married to

Alex, her beauty-therapy business is flourishing, and she and Alex are considering starting a family. Maria's artistic talents have also blossomed far beyond a hobby. She is a talented painter in her own right, often painting on commission. While she maintains contact with her father, she is estranged from both her mother and sister. To them, she is a pariah, a fallen Witness, forever tainted and doomed.

Maria, though, has discovered her own nirvana, and it didn't take the 'end of days' to get there – just a brave, determined decision to leave the Jehovah's Witnesses and start again: 'In my husband I found the most incredible person. I cherish and admire him every single day of my life. He has been the driving force in helping me believe in myself and in humanity once again. His love and support are worth more to me than anything I could ever possibly wish for. I thank him from the bottom of my heart for everything he is and the love he gives me. What a beautiful life we now have, and I can truly say I have found my happy ending.'

References

Abrahams, K. (2009). *I'm Perfect, You're Doomed: Tales from a Jehovah's Witness Upbringing*. New York, NY: Touchstone

Augustine, J. (15 November 2018). The Watchtower Bible & Tract Society: $1.45 Billion in Assets. Retrieved from: https://scientologymoneyproject.com/2018/11/15/the-watchtower-bible-tract-society-1-45-billion-in-assets/

Avery, D. (14 August 2019). New Law Could Open Floodgates on Decades of Child Sexual Abuse Within Jehovah's Witnesses. *Newsweek*. Retrieved from: https://www.newsweek.com/jehovahs-witnesses-child-sex-abuse-lawsuit-1453610#:~:text=Tech-,New%20Law%20Could%20Open%20Floodgates%20on%20Decades,Sexual%20Abuse%20Within%20Jehovah's%20Witnesses&text=It%20can%20take%20years%2C%20even,them%20with%20no%20legal%20recourse

Baldas, T. (20 March 2018). Ex-Jehovah's Witnesses Break Silence on Shunning: 'My Mother Treats Me Like I'm Dead'. *USA Today Online*. Retrieved from: www.usatoday.com/story/news/nation-now/2018/03/20/jehovahs-witnesses-shunning-disfellowship-suicides/438499002

BBC Bitesize. Nature of Jesus in Christianity. Retrieved from: https://www.bbc.co.uk/bitesize/guides/z43f3k7/revision/2

Bundy, T. (21 March 2018). Jehovah's Witnesses Abuse Files Remain Secret After Court Settlements. *Reveal News*. Retrieved from: https://revealnews.org/blog/jehovahs-witness-abuse-files-remain-secret-after-court-settlements/

Catholic Answers. History of the Jehovah's Witnesses. *Catholic Answers*.

Chuck, E. (7 October 2018). Jehovah's Witnesses 'Use the Bible to Victim-Shame', Sex Abuse Survivor Says. *NBC News*. Retrieved from: https://www.nbcnews.com/news/us-news/jehovah-s-witnesses-use-bible-victim-shame-sex-abuse-survivor-n916326

Clark, D. (2007). *I, Witness: The Shocking Insider's Story of Jehovah's Witnesses*. Englewood, CO: Villa Press

Cox, R. (January 2010). The Jehovah's Witness Experience. *American Annals of the Deaf.* 155(4): 517–517. Retrieved from: https://www.researchgate.net/publication/265756113_The_Jehovah's_Witness_Experience

Criscione, W. (18 October 2022). Jehovah's Witness Church Covered Up Child Sex Abuse, Survivors Say. *Crosscut*. Retrieved from: https://crosscut.com/news/2022/10/jehovahs-witness-church-covered-child-sex-abuse-survivors-say

Cutler, M. and K. Conley. (2022). *Cults: Inside the World's Most Notorious Groups and Understanding the People Who Joined Them*. New York, NY: Gallery Books

Davis, K. (6 March 2018). San Diego Sex Abuse Cases Against Jehovah's Witness Organization Settled. *The San Diego Union Tribune*. Retrieved from: https://www.sandiegouniontribune.com/news/courts/sd-me-jehovahs-witness-20180306-story.html

_______. (14 April 2016). $13.5M Award Vacated in Jehovah's Witness Abuse Case. *The San Diego Union Tribune*. Retrieved from: www.sandiegounion tribune.com/sdut-jehovahs-witness-lopez-sex-abuse-appeal-2016apr14-htmlstory.html

Dickson, E.J. (22 March 2019). Jehovah's Witnesses Accused of Mishandling Child Sexual Abuse Claims. *Rolling Stone* magazine. Retrieved from: https://www.rollingstone.com/culture/culture-news/jehovahs-witnesses-child-sexual-abuse-811927/

Evans, L. (2017). *The Reluctant Apostate: Leaving Jehovah's Witnesses Comes at a Price*. Cheshire, England: JLE Publishing

_______. (2018). *How to Escape from Jehovah's Witnesses*. Cheshire, England: JLE Publishing

Farmer, B. (26 April 2023). Jehovah's Witness Leaders Win Supreme Court Appeal After Woman Raped by Elder. *Independent UK*. Retrieved from: https://www.independent.co.uk/news/uk/crime/supreme-court-witness-high-court-court-of-appeal-cardiff-b2327200.html

Fautre, W. (2012). Cults and Religious Freedom Around the World. ICSA Annual International Conference: Manipulation and Victimization, Montreal, Canada. 5-7 July 2012. Retrieved from: https://www.academia.edu/5201173/Cult_Issues_and_Religious_Freedom

Foss, K. (20 February 2009). Court Saves Jehovah's Witness Girl's Life. *IOL*. Retrieved from: https://www.iol.co.za/news/south-africa/court-saves-jehovahs-witness-girls-life-435180

Guinn, J. (2017). *The Road to Jonestown: Jim Jones and Peoples Temple*. New York, NY: Simon & Schuster

Hargrove, D. (12 January 2018). Jehovah's Witnesses to Settle Sex-Abuse Case. *San Diego Reader*. Retrieved from: www.sandiegoreader.com/news/2018/jan/12/ticker-jehovahs-witnesses-settle-sex-abuse-case

Hartley-Parkinson, R., and M. Duell. (10 July 2015). 'I Would Do It Again 100 Times': Muslim Father 'Murdered His Three Daughters in Honour Killing for Dating Wrong Boys'. *Daily Mail Online*. Retrieved from: www.dailymail.co.uk/news/article-2061842/Mohammad-Shafia-murdered-daughter-honour-killing-said-hed-again.html

Hassan, S.A. (5 June 2021). Understanding Cults: The Basics. *Psychology Today*. Retrieved from: https://www.psychologytoday.com/us/blog/freedom-mind/202106/understanding-cults-the-basics

__________. (1990). *Combating Cult Mind Control*. Rochester, Vermont: Park Street Press

__________. (2000). *Releasing the Bonds*. Newton, MA: Freedom of Mind Press

Hicks, A. (26 September 2018). Three Jehovah's Witnesses Who Feared End of the World was Coming Fled Home Naked and Kidnapped Neighbours. *The Mirror Online*. Retrieved from: https://www.mirror.co.uk/news/world-news/

James, A. (2013). *'Knock Knock' Who's There? 'The Truth' About Jehovah's Witnesses*. Scotts Valley, California: CreateSpace Independent Publishing Platform

Jehovah's Witnesses official website: www.JW.org

Jones, C. (4 February 2020). Jehovah's Witnesses Sued Over 'Historical Sex Abuse'. *BBC News: Victoria Derbyshire* programme. Retrieved from: https://www.bbc.com/news/uk-51006771

Lifton, R.J. (2014). *Thought Reform and the Psychology of Totalism: A Study of Brainwashing in China*. Connecticut, New England: Martino Fine Books

Marcus, J. (12 November 2020). Jehovah's Witness Elders Made Teen Listen [to] Recording of Her Rape for Hours, Lawsuit Claims. *Independent News*. Retrieved from: www.independent.co.uk/news/world/americas/jehovahs-witnesses-rape-first-amendment-utah-b1722138.html

Marsh, S. (25 March 2018). Jehovah's Witnesses Accused of Silencing Victims of Child Abuse. *The Guardian*. Retrieved from: https://www.theguardian.com/world/2018/mar/25/jehovahs-witnesses-accused-of-silencing-victims-of-child-abuse-uk

Martin, D. (19 August 2014). Sangoma. *Encyclopaedia Britannica*. Retrieved from: https://www.britannica.com/science/sangoma

Mehta, H. (31 January 2022). Norway Will No Longer Fund the Jehovah's Witnesses. *OnlySky Media*. Retrieved from: https://onlysky.media/hemant-mehta/norway-will-no-longer-fund-the-jehovahs-witnesses/

Melton, J.G. (2 December 2022). Jehovah's Witness. *Encyclopaedia Britannica.* Retrieved from: https://www.britannica.com/topic/Jehovahs-Witnesses

Melton, J.G., and J.H. Smylie. (25 August 2022). Adventist. *Encyclopaedia Britannica.* Retrieved from: https://www.britannica.com/topic/Adventism

Miller, K.L. (2021). *To Go Beneath the Water*. California, United States: More Than Words Publishing

Mkhwanazi, S. (10 July 2006). Father to Answer Charges of Rape and Incest. *IOL*. Retrieved from: https://www.iol.co.za/news/south-africa/father-to-answer-charges-of-rape-and-incest-284811

Newcombe, S. (November 2014). Cults: History, Beliefs, Practices. In Terry Muck, Harold A. Netland, and Gerald R. McDermott (eds). *Handbook of Religion: A Christian Engagement with Traditions, Teachings, and Practices.* London: Baker Academic, pp. 568–572

Nivashni, N. (26 February 2019). Jehovah's Witness Parents Prevent Blood Transfusions for Three Children. *TimesLIVE*. Retrieved from: https://www.timeslive.co.za/news/south-africa/2019-02-26-jehovahs-witness-parents-prevent-blood-transfusions-for--three-children/

Osborne, S. (10 January 2018). Ex-Jehovah's Witness Reveals Secrets of Religious Group. *The Independent*. Retrieved from: https://www.independent.co.uk/news/uk/home-news/jehovahs-witnesses-religion-christianity-religious-group-what-is-it-like-a7214966.html

Osuh, C. (26 July 2017). Jehovah's Witnesses Criticised by Charity Commission Over Handling of Sex Abuse Case. *Manchester Evening News*. Retrieved from: https://www.manchestereveningnews.co.uk/news/greater-manchester-news/jehovahs-witnesses-criticised-charity-commission-13391368

Parry, H. (13 December 2015). Jehovah's Witnesses Set to Make $1billion by Selling Off Their New York City Watchtower Headquarters. *Mail Online*. Retrieved from: https://www.dailymail.co.uk/news/article-3358416/Jehovah-s-Witnesses-set-make-1billion-selling-iconic-New-York-City-Watchtower-headquarters

Post, K. (27 October 2022). Four Jehovah's Witnesses Charged with Sexual Abuse of 19 Children Across Pennsylvania. *Religion News Service*. Retrieved from: https://religionnews.com/2022/10/27/four-jehovahs-witnesses-charged-for-sexual-abuse-of-19-children-across-pennsylvania/

Prudêncio, N. (14 February 2023). More Than 4,800 Cases of Sexual Abuse Within the Catholic Church Uncovered in Portugal. *Euronews* Online. Retrieved from: https://www.euronews.com/2023/02/14/more-than-4800-cases-of-sexual-abuse-within-the-catholic-church-uncovered-in-portugal

Quenqua, D. (22 March 2019). A Secret Database of Child Abuse. *The Atlantic*. Retrieved from: https://www.theatlantic.com/family/archive/2019/03/the-secret-jehovahs-witness-database-of-child-molesters/584311/

Quora. Do Jehovah's Witnesses Profit from Disaster Relief? Retrieved from: https://www.quora.com/Do-Jehovahs-Witnesses-profit-from-disaster-relief

RadioFree Europe/RadioLiberty. (7 February 2019). Countries Where Jehovah's Witnesses' Activities Are Banned. Retrieved from: https://www.rferl.org/a/countries-where-jehovahs-witnesses-activities-are-banned/29757419.html

Robehmed, S. (8 July 2014). The Jehovah's Witnesses' New Tactic. *BBC News*. Retrieved from: https://www.bbc.com/news/magazine-28166192

Rodia, T. (29 August 2019). Is It a Cult or a New Religious Movement? *Penn Today*. Retrieved from: http://penntoday.upenn.edu/news/it-cult-or-new-religious-movement.

Ross, A. (12 August 2016). Jehovah's Witnesses Under Pressure Over Handling of Sexual Abuse Claims. *The Guardian*. Retrieved from: https://www.theguardian.com/society/2016/aug/12/jehovahs-witnesses-under-pressure-over-handling-of-sexual-abuse-claims#:~:text=Jehovah's%20Witnesses%20under%20pressure%20over%20handling%20of%20sexual%20abuse%20claims,-This%20article%20is&text=The%20Jehovah's%20Witnesses%20organisation%20is,its%20records%20of%20abuse%20claims

Schmidt, N., J. Gretener, T. John, and C. Lau. (10 March 2023). Deadly Mass Shooting at Jehovah's Witnesses Center in Hamburg Stuns Germany. *CNN World News Online*. Retrieved from: https://www.cnn.com/2023/03/10/europe/hamburg-germany-shooting-intl

Sherwood, H. (10 August 2020). Former Jehovah's Witness Elders Call for Mandatory Reporting of Child Sexual Abuse. Retrieved from: https://www.theguardian.com/world/2020/aug/10/former-jehovahs-witness-elders-call-for-mandatory-reporting-of-child-sexual-abuse

Siegel, M. (27 July 2015). Jehovah's Witnesses Hid Child Sex Abuse Cases: Australian Inquiry Told. *Reuters*. Retrieved from: https://www.reuters.com/article/us-australia-religion-sexcrimes-idUSKCN0Q10IH20150727

Soriano, M. (25 July 2017). The Ex-Jehovah's Witnesses Shunned by Their Families. *BBC News – Victoria Derbyshire* programme. Retrieved from: https://www.bbc.com/news/uk-40704990

Study.com. Jehovah's Witnesses: History, Founder & Church. Retrieved from: https://study.com/academy/lesson/jehovahs-witnesses-origin-founder-history.html

Symonds, T. (2 September 2021). Religious Groups in UK Failing Children Over Sexual Abuse, Report Says. *BBC News*. Retrieved from: https://www.bbc.com/news/uk-58420270

Walsh, R. (2013). *The Day of Jehovah's Witnesses*. Colchester, England: Spiffing Covers Publishing

Additional Sources:

Assisting Victims of Ostracism, Injustice, and Deceit in Jehovah's Witnesses. GERMANY: Child Sexual Abuse in Jehovah's Witnesses. Retrieved from: https://avoidjw.org/legal/germany-child-sexual-abuse-in-jehovahs-witnesses/

Four Corners (2021). Escaping Jehovah's Witnesses: Inside the Dangerous World of a Brutal Religion. *ABC News In-depth*. Retrieved from: https://www.youtube.com/watch?v=gDwHdj7plWo

Royal Commission into Institutional Responses to Child Sexual Abuse. (28 November 2016). Report in Jehovah's Witness Organisations Released. Retrieved from: www.childabuseroyalcommission.gov.au/media-releases/report-jehovahs-witness-organisations-released

____________. (October 2016). Report of Case Study No. 29: The Response of the Jehovah's Witnesses and Watchtower Bible and Tract Society Australia Ltd. to Allegations of Child Sexual Abuse. Retrieved from: https://nla.gov.au/nla.obj-541699262/view